T0207872

CHUANG TZU'S
"CRAZY WISDOM"
FOR ELDERS

DONALD P. ST. JOHN

BALBOA.
PRESS

A DIVISION OF HAY HOUSE

Balboa Press books may be ordered through booksellers or by contacting:

Balboa Press
A Division of Hay House
1663 Liberty Drive
Bloomington, IN 47403
www.balboapress.com
1 (877) 407-4847

Excerpts from *Chuang Tzu: The Inner Chapters*, translated by A.C. Graham, copyright 1981, 1986,1989 by A.C. Graham. Reprinted by permission of Hackett Publishing Co., Inc. Indianapolis.

Excerpts from *The Way of Chuang Tzu* by Thomas Merton. Copyrighted 1965 by The Abbey of Gethsemani. Reprinted by permission of New Directions Publishing Corp., New York.

Print information available on the last page.

ISBN: 978-1-9822-3625-0 (sc)
ISBN: 978-1-9822-3626-7 (e)

Balboa Press rev. date: 10/11/2019

CONTENTS

PREFACE

The range of courses in global religions and philosophies for which some academics in small liberal arts colleges are responsible, invites them to continue expanding and deepening their knowledge, especially of traditions that they did not focus on during graduate school. To do this, they rely mostly on the expertise of western scholars who, while translating and analyzing ancient texts, also provide the political, cultural and historical background for texts such as the ancient Chinese *Tao te Ching/daodejing* and the *Chuang Tzu/Zhuangzi*. My own understanding of and appreciation for ancient Taoism/Daoism was enriched by a wonderful group of nineteenth to twenty-first century Sinologists like Graham, Watson, Waltham and Legge, Roth, Ivanhoe, Mair, Chan, and Girardot. They, along with contemplatives such as Thomas Merton, helped enrich my sensitivity to the spiritual depths of these traditions. I was also struck by the interlocking patterns, webs of associations, and symbolic similarities among phenomena in different traditions.

Recently, I became fascinated with works on aging and ageism. They called to mind the critical as well as creative spirit of the 1960s with its civil rights and feminist causes. For example, the narratives and reflections by over 100 elders who participated in Eugene C. Bianchi's *Wisdom Project* were a rich source for his landmark work, *Elder Wisdom: Creating Your Own Elderhood* (Crossroad, 1994). In the writings of Margaret Cruikshank, especially her *Learning to be Old: Gender, Culture, and Aging* (Rowan & Littlefield, 2013), I found powerful analyses and critiques of the conventional views on aging and the socio-economic and cultural influences that supported the current prejudices and narrow stereotypes. This is also true of Margaret M. Gullette's *Agewise: Fighting The New Ageism in America, Aging as Saging* by Rabbi Zalman Schacter, *Contemplative Aging* by Edmund Sherman, *The Art of Aging* by Sherwin Nuland, the groundbreaking work, *What Are Old People For?* by William Thomas, M.D. The Franciscan Richard Rohr's *Falling Upward: A Spirituality for the Two Halves of Life* and more recently, the Benedictine nun Joan Chittister's *The Gift of Years*, provide not only critiques of many shallow and/or negative views concerning elders but, more importantly, counter these with positive insights on elders and their unique potential for personal growth. Given my penchant for seeing patterns connecting diverse cultural phenomena, I was excited that many of these works resonated with the philosophical, religious and spiritual works I was continuing to study, to teach and to write about.

I was especially startled and excited when I began to realize that the probing insights of the ancient Taoists/Daoists, especially the philosopher and storyteller Chuang Tzu/Zhuangzi (ca, 370-286 b.c.e.) were relevant in a very fruitful way to the current attempts to address many of the issues surrounding the emerging population of elders and to deepen our understanding of what the wisdom of an elder can be (even if thought "crazy" by adults). It was in the creative and timeless work of Chuang Tzu/Zhuangzi that I found a myriad of unconventional individuals who, by their actions as well as their clever insights, offered ways (taos/daos) to develop, bring to expression and humanize (even humorize) the hidden potentials of elders.

The individuals through whom the *Chuang Tzu* (title of the written work) presents its unorthodox wisdom into the ancient (and modern) Chinese world were often judged by defenders of the Confucian world to be a bit "crazy," often "odd" and unorthodox, both in physical appearance and behavior (like the modern judgments made about many elders). In the *Chuang Tzu,* not coincidentally, these are often elders though sometimes younger adults or children.

The *Chuang Tzu* uses both common and paradoxical expressions to reveal uncommon modes of knowing, doing, and being, Some of these words, such as "forgetting" and "wandering," are used today to glibly, even sarcastically, characterize and put-down certain qualities and behaviors associated with elders. But Chuang Tzu shows how these experiences, instead of signaling the beginning of a downturn in mental or physical capacities, can be used to help elders and older adults identify and initiate positive "ways" to grow, guided and energized by individual potentials that have been hidden, undeveloped or underdeveloped.

> Note: As you notice, I use two romanized spellings of the philosopher's name: Chuang Tzu and Zhuangzi. The former was the dominant way to place Mandarin Chinese into western spelling and pronunciation until the latter half of the twentieth century. It is called the Wade-Giles system while the now dominant romanized spelling for transliterating Chinese based more closely

on the Chinese pronunciation of letters and words is the Pinyin. First the Wade-Giles then the Pinyin spelling will be used when I introduce a word, e.g. Chuang Tzu/Zhuangzi, hsin/xin, jen/ren. Later my choice will depend on which system the western translator or scholar on whom I am basing my reflections uses (with some exceptions based on my own "crazy" intuition). At the end of this book I will list some key terms with both their Wade-Giles and Pinyin romanized spellings.

INTRODUCTION

I

MODERN RE-SEARCHING AND RE-THINKING OF ELDERHOOD

Researcher Laura Carstesen, at the end of a study of emotional development across the adult lifespan, concludes:

> Development brings increasing differentiation. We found greater differentiation in emotional experience in older as compared to younger people, and we found that emotional differentiation is related to a positive profile of characteristics, including less neuroticism and better emotional control . . . At the same time in life when cognitive speed and biological hardiness are on

the decline, emotional functioning may continue to
improve. (in Thomas, 27)

Reviewing this and other studies, William Thomas, M.D. concludes
that the "emotional dimension of old age is vast and remains little
understood" (Thomas, 27). If we can free ourselves "from the
presumption of decline, we can begin to explore new ideas and concepts
that can illuminate age and aging in modern society" (Ibid.). I have
found *What Are Old People For?* by Dr. Thomas to be of great value in
terms of an analysis of popular and even some professional half-truths
concerning "Old People." Research gerontologist (and philosopher and
psychologist) Edmund Sherman cites "substantial research findings
showing distinct differences in temperament and personality over
the lifespan," concluding that "there is no *one* way to *be* in later life
(Sherman, 38).

Unfortunately, our society is dominated by what is known in gerontology
and other fields as a "functionalist" ethos and ethic. According to
Sherman, this "is an ethic by which the person evaluates his or her *self*
worth in terms of his or her functional value in society" (Sherman, 37).
Given that modern society places such a high value "on the production
and consumption of goods and services…" a person is "evaluated in
terms of productive, professional, or service functioning, monetary
worth and the quantity and quality of goods and services consumed in
a market economy" (Ibid.).

In Sherman's own study, in fact, over half of the elders interviewed,
"identified with and evaluated themselves in terms of the functionalist
ethic" (Sherman, 37). For elders influenced by this ethos, the period
known as "retirement" can signal a crisis in identity and in one's
sense of self-worth. Questions like "who am I aside from my career

or job?" or "what should I do?" or "what will make life worthwhile?" trouble many elders. Regrettably, "the highly socialized view inherent in the functionalist ethic simply does not allow for the uniqueness of individuals, especially in later life" (Sherman, 39).

But, as we shall see, the ancient Taoist/Daoist philosopher Chuang Tzu/ Zhuangzi offers his readers a number of unique, often "odd" individuals, considered "strange" by conventional adult standards, but who turn out to be filled with sagely wisdom both in heart and mind (heart/ mind). Chuang Tzu frequently fills his stories and pithy dialogues with a healthy dose of humor that subtly, and often not so subtly, challenges the overly serious yet narrow Confucian views and values penetrating the lives of its ordinary members as well as its philosophical and political spokespersons. Reading and reflecting on the *Chuang Tzu* can help a contemporary elder liberate his or her mind/heart (*hsin/xin*) from modern society's narrow views and values and develop a vision and sense of self based on the emergence of their own under-realized qualities.

As James Hillman points out in his book, *The Force of Character: And the Lasting Life*, "Character! Character governs . . . That specific composition of traits, foibles, delights, and commitments" that identify the figure bearing our name, our history and the face that mirrors 'me' (1999, p.7, in Sherman, 58). As Sherman, echoing Hillman states: "To be unique as a character is to be odd, atypical, and different" (Sherman, 58). As far as the unique and atypical qualities of our own individual character are concerned, Chuang Tzu's "characters" should encourage us to explore and then embrace them as expressions of our own deeper reality (te/de) which itself emerges from a yet deeper and wider Source and Process.

Many elders intuitively sense that there is more to them than what the functionalist ethos purports. Here is where an alternative can be of great value for the fuller development of each elder's *being* (who they *are*, not simply what they *do*). Hopefully, exposure to the wisdom of Chuang Tzu/Zhuangzi will, 1) foster a desire by elders to nurture the growth of their deeper qualities, 2) assist those seeking to develop more contemplative and poetic ways of knowing self, others and the Earth, and 3) encourage elders to become involved with young people and help them to recognize and move away from the conformist pressures of adult educational and social indoctrination and towards a more genuinely personal self-realization. Finally, elders will also find that Chuang Tzu's vision and values (as well as those of Lieh Tzu/Lizi, another Taoist) draw them towards non-violent ways of living-and-doing that are supportive of a common yet diverse human-earth community out of which they emerged and back into which they will return.

II

CHUANG WHO?

Chinese Taoist/Daoist philosopher Chuang Tzu/Zhuangzi (ca.370-286 b.c.e.) set about to shake up conventional assumptions and up-set the set minds of the people of his day. In puncturing many of the intellectual balloons held by political, social and intellectual leaders, Master (Tzu) Chuang employed bold, humorous and frequently outlandish tales and tactics, vehicles of what is known as "crazy wisdom." Realizing how stories stick in people's minds, he used stories to un-stick lazily acquired prejudices and conventions. He did not do this to leave people in a state of mental or ethical confusion, but to liberate their *hsin/xin* (mind/ heart or mind/spirit) from the shackles of conventional stereotypes so that their *xin* could be free to develop and explore deeper ways (*taos/*

daos) of being, seeing, knowing, and doing. As the Daoist/Taoist work *Lieh Tzu(Lizi)* (ca.200A.D.) expresses it: "My body is in accord with my mind, my mind with my energies, my energies with my spirit, my spirit with Nothing" (Graham, 1990, p.77). "Nothing" signifies the deepest Reality for Chuang Tzu and Lieh Tzu. It is not a thing but no-thing, not an object but a deep all-pervading Reality, the Way (Tao).

Obviously, such a transformation would be difficult for people of his time and ours if Chuang Tzu had simply argued his case at the level and with the terminology of an abstract epistemology and metaphysics. Fortunately, however, Chuang Tzu offers a treasure trove of stories and tales that can provide us with wisdom originating, indwelling and expressed by scores of "crazy" and sometimes bizarre women and men.

On initial contact, especially by convinced followers of the intellectual or social elite like Confucius, Chuang Tzu's "characters," many of whom were "elders," seemed to have challenged the popular image and expectations of what it took to be considered a Sage. Yet a depth of mind, heart and vital energy/spirit lay beneath their frequently unusual physical appearances and behaviors. This intuitive truth was quickly and surprisingly realized by Confucius and others of his social stature in the *Chuang Tzu*, where they often appear quite Daoist. But often, once revealed, this wisdom would stir something inside the sensitively intelligent person and stoke a desire to become a student or disciple of this unusual sage. They would realize that it was time to move to another level of being and maybe even to another society.

As Taoist scholar Philip J. Ivanhoe notes, "One can neither flee from one's culture nor succumb to it but instead must learn how to live in it but not be of it" (Ivanhoe, 88). In order "to avoid or undo the deleterious effects of socialization," one "must undergo a process of self-cultivation." The dynamic of this process seeks to undo the "effects of society's pernicious influences," thus allowing us to "get back in touch with our spontaneous inclinations and orientations" and to permit us to "gradually inform and guide our attitudes and actions" (Ivanhoe, 88,89).

Hopefully, Chuang Tzu/Zhuangzi can assist today's elders in freeing themselves from the power of negative stereotypes and in opening themselves to the transforming influence of their own inner powers. When initiated, self-cultivation will allow an elder to experience and nurture his or her "spontaneous, pre-reflective inclinations," developing them in a way that can open their mind/heart or mind/ spirit so as to touch another level. Perhaps elders will "wander" about mentally and physically even as the gatekeepers of Adult society criticize their wandering mind or body and attempt to close the gates on both. As Ivanhoe notes, "[i]n Zhuangzi's terms, one must learn to 'walk without touching the ground' and 'fly without wings'" (Ivanhoe, 88). Crazy wisdom.

It is our hope, in short, that through this work we can: 1) contribute to a recognition of modern society's uncreative stereotypes and often biased views concerning the meaning of aging and of being an elder, 2) suggest ways by which elders could free themselves both mentally and emotionally from these external and often internalized social, cultural and psychological bonds, 3) demonstrate ways (*taos/daos*) by which elders can explore, engage with and be energized by an integrated functioning of body, heart-mind, and spirit or spiritual energy (*shenqi*), and 4) help elders (and others) develop an appreciation for and sensitivity to the dynamic, harmonious and diverse unity of the wider cosmic-earth process as well as to learn how to move with it, and thus be inspired and energized in a variety of concrete ways (*daos*).

III

Why Stories?

One final note may be in order. It is no coincidence that the *Chuang Tzu* utilized stories, jokes, humorous anecdotes and some sharp logical barbs to open the mind-heart or mind-spirit *(xin)* of his hearer/reader so that they might experience directly the often complex and subtle sources of moral insight and spiritual experience. The Ecofeminist Karen Warren points out that the validity of an approach to truth and meaning that "grows out of, and is faithful to, felt, lived experience" has often been rejected by many mainstream philosophers of East and West (in Pojman, 595). That is because it utilizes narrative to get to and adequately convey these living truths and meanings. Rather than have agents who impose abstract principles upon concrete situations in which they find themselves, narrative "provides a way of conceiving of ethical [and other] meaning as *emerging out of* particular situations moral agents find themselves in ..." (Ibid).

Narrative also requires that the reader be sensitive to *voice*, including the diversity of voices arising out of and reflecting differences in culture, gender, race, history, etc. (in Pojman, 595). Given the diverse and unconventional characters whose voices are heard and deeds are described in the *Chuang Tzu*, attentive sensitivity to a variety of voices operating within complex settings with ongoing dialogues and discussions, is essential to grasping and appreciating meaning. Faithful to the rich narrative style of most of the *Chuang Tzu*, we will stay close to the philosopher's stories and humorous anecdotes in order both to demonstrate their relevance as sources for rethinking modern elderhood and to allow the reader an opportunity to discover and develop his or her own "crazy wisdom".

WORKS CITED

Carr, Karen L. and Philip Ivanhoe, *The Sense of Antirationalism: The Religious Thought of Zhuangzi and Kierkegaard,* rev. edition, CreativeSpace Independent Publishing Platform, 2010

Carstensen, Laura L., et. al. "Emotional Experience in Everyday Life Across the Adult Lifespan," *Journal of Personality and Social Psychology* 79 no. 4 (2000): 644-655.

Graham, A.C., *The Book of Lieh-Tzu.* New York: Columbia University Press, 1990.

Hillman, James. *The Force of Character: And the Lasting Life.* New York: Random House,1999.

Sherman, Edmund. *Contemplative Aging: A Way of Being in Later Life.* Surrey: Gordian Knot Books, 2010.

Steinberg, Laurence. "The Case for Delayed Adulthood," *New York Times*, September 21, 2014, p 12.

Thomas, William H. *What Are Old People For? How Elders Will Save the World*. Acton, MA: VanderWyk and Burnham, 2004.

Warren, Karen J. "The Power and Promise of Ecological Feminism." In *Environmental Ethics: Readings in Theory and Application*, 6th Edition edited by Paul and Louis Pojman, 589-605. Belmont: CA: Thomson Wadsworth, 2012.

CHAPTER ONE

Of Covers and Books

To the extent that the physical appearance of elders contrasts with the dominant American image of what is "normal" and "appealing," people respond to them with a mix of pity, negative judgment, and self-referential anxiety. Obsessed with surface appearances, popular culture ignores the deeper and more valuable qualities that mark us as persons. Anybody, including elders, with a misshapen, unusual or "physically challenged" appearance can be considered a threat to the norm. And this prejudice against those who seem crippled, "deformed," or "differently shaped" in body, applies also to the wrinkled face and graying hair. These cultural biases make it very difficult for people to see beyond superficial appearances. Hence they remain blind to what is actually there in front of their eyes.

Unfortunately, many elders have internalized their culture's biases. They look into the mirror wearing the same culturally faulty lenses. They become embarrassed or depressed by their own image. It is one thing when the "duped" make superficial judgments about elders; it is another when the latter do it to themselves. Instead of freeing themselves from Blake's "mind-forg'd manacles," they foolishly waste money and energy, trouble their minds and hearts, and tighten these "manacles" in the chase after the illusive promises made by anti-aging gurus and their products. Instead of learning to listen to their unique call to the elder vocation and to become sensitive to their own inner creative Powers (de/*te*), they walk around haunted by images of beauty and health and vibrancy created by adultworld.

Chuang Tzu challenged the similarly conventional, superficial and often cruel judgments of the people of his day. Instead of following the custom of his time and portraying the paragons of wisdom and inner power with flawless skin, erect posture and perfect health, his sages and heroes were often fractured, misshapen, or twisted. Ostracized, ridiculed or simply ignored by the superficial denizens of conventional taste, these denigrated "others" turned out to be infinitely more interesting and spiritually more powerful than their pretentious critics. In fact, Chuang Tzu's stories challenge us to break loose and free our ordinary minds from all internalized biases so that we might open our deeper minds to the richness of what is before us (and within us). Freeing ourselves from the judgments of others can also free us from many of the judgments we make about ourselves and thereby free us to more deeply explore the question of who we really are.

I

You Can't Tell A Book By Its Cover

Chapter Five of the *Chuang Tzu/Zhuangzi,* contains many stories featuring characters whose appearances are considered misshapen, ugly, "physically challenged" or just "different." In section 4, we meet an extremely ugly and misshapen man named Nag the Hump (Mair) or Uglyface T'o (Graham). Nag seemed to possess few of the abilities, little of the prowess, and none of the features admired by others, and yet they competed for his friendship. Despite the widespread availability of handsome or at least tolerably attractive men, young women begged their parents to allow them to become Nag's concubine rather than take any of the "normal" men for their husbands. The ruler Duke Ai of Lu was so taken with Nag that he offered him the position of Prime Minister and soon entrusted him with his entire kingdom. The Duke confessed that Nag was extremely inarticulate and "ugly enough to terrify all under heaven" (Mair, 46). When Nag unexpectedly quit his post, the Duke was inconsolable. He sought out Confucius and begged him to explain what made Nag so irresistible.

Confucius began by recalling when, in the state of Ch'u, he saw piglets trying to suckle at their dead mother. They soon abandoned her, however, because they no longer recognized something of themselves in her. The little pigs were drawn to her by what animated her and not by her physical form. When that force departed, so did they. Similarly, people sense Nag's inner power and peacefulness and are drawn to him because his presence awakens a peacefulness and spiritual power within themselves. Likewise, Confucius opines, a dead soldier, absent life, makes no demands for funeral plumes and a person absent his feet, has no desire for shoes. Confucius suggests that Nag's appeal comes from an inner wholeness that exercises a mysterious "influence" over others.

Confucius concludes that Nag's Virtue (*de/te*) is whole and complete despite his imperfect and flawed outward appearance and ways of acting. Ironically, Confucianists themselves, of course, emphasized the Gentleman's (*junzi/chun tzu*) impressive physical bearing, eloquence of speech, appropriate tone of voice, respectful facial expressions and graceful gestures. All of these would be tastefully coordinated with customary ritual behavior (*li*). Yet, Confucius himself praises a quality or power that emanates from within and does not require an externally dignified or aesthetically pleasing bearing to have a good influence on other individuals and a harmonizing influence on society. In short, Nag models himself on and influences others with the power or virtue (*de/te*) of the Way (*Dao/Tao*).

Confucius is pressed to talk more about this inner power and wholeness. The Master points out that life in its myriad forms is constantly changing. In addition, conditions and events come and go that are frequently beyond one's control: birth and death, success and failure, poverty and wealth, repute and disrepute. A person such as Nag does not allow these changes to disturb his equanimity or rob him of the spiritual riches securely stored within. He remains centered even as he flexibly moves with and is present to these changes.

Poetically, Confucius explains that even as the seasons come and go, it is always springtime in Nag's heart. His inner spirit remains full amidst outer transformations, even death. Confucius states that Nag is a person whose abilities are whole but whose integrity is "not evident in his physical form" (Mair, 47).

Speaking of "integrity" (te/de), Confucius uses water, a favorite symbol of Taoists, to characterize Integrity as central to the growth and dynamism of all other personal and cosmic qualities. Just as water at rest is "level," so our inner life can be unruffled and at peace. Through cultivating it within we will avoid being ruffled without. According to Chuang Tzu's Confucius, one should cultivate a mind that is "placid and free-flowing," that moves with life's unfolding but is not "dissipated in gratification" (Mair, 48). (This may imply that for the elder there is no need to try to artificially cling to or recapture the appearances of youth). It means having "springtime" in our hearts and in our relationship with others, through day and night, summer and winter. We become "indispensable to all things" (Mair, 48).

Carrying "constant springtime" in one's heart and mind allows it to permeate one's body. Confucius explains that this is what he means when he explains that the "wholeness of one's abilities" is present in Nag (Ibid.).

The Duke suddenly realizes that Nag's spirituality might hold the key to his own desire to be a more successful leader. Perhaps he would exercise more influence over his countrymen and stimulate harmony in society if he cultivated and nurtured his own inner life and powers.

This, of course, is the traditional "Way" of the Daoist ruler as found, for example, in the *Tao te Ching/Daodejing*. Hence, the incredible influence of Ugly Misshapen Nag is due to an invisible influence that he exercises on everyone around him. As they are drawn towards him, they feel an urge to develop their own inner lives. Why couldn't a ruler do the same thing? (Or, we might ask, an elder?) Wise elders learn to identify and then activate the inner resources and spiritual qualities that will allow them to remain calm with equanimity even amidst constant and at times threatening change. This special quality of elders can enable them to contribute positively to the efforts of young people to create new Green movements while dealing with opposition of all sorts from all quarters.

II

When The Book Remakes the Cover

Let us reflect on another story from Chapter Five. Here we meet a person named Lipless Clubfoot Scattered (Mair) or Mr. Lame-Hunchback-No-Lips (Watson) whose inner power or integrity (*de*) is so strong that not only do people forget his unattractive "physical form" but change their own criteria for judging beauty and attractiveness. When men such as Lipless Clubfoot Scattered (Mair) or Mr. Pitcher-Sized Wen (Watson) spoke with Dukes of different states, the latter thought the necks of normal people to be "too lean and skinny" (Watson, 71). People of "normal" or even "superior" physical qualities are now considered terribly lacking. Instead of the book being judged by its cover, the cover is now judged by the book.

Those labeled as physically odd, ugly or misshapen become attractive alternatives to the blandness of conventional "beauty." The majority adopt a character-istic of the minority that indicates that they are also spiritually deep and mature and hence worthy of adulation. To *look* like the "other" suggests that you *are* like them, that is, whole and spiritually attractive. You have risen above the superficial and narrow-minded judgments of the masses. And in such a world, might not the impressive efficacy of the spiritual qualities of elders create a new standard? For Chuang Tzu, if people forget what they usually do not forget, [their obsession with appearances] and do not forget what they usually forget [that is, to nurture their inner qualities] "that may be called true forgetting" (Watson, 71).

III

Discrimination and the Logic of Domination

In Section 2 of Chapter Five, we meet two students of a Daoist Master, Sir Ch'an. One is the prime minster of Cheng, and the other is Shen-t'u Chia, a cripple (Mair, 44-45). As one might expect, the prime minister did not feel comfortable being placed on an equal "footing" with a low class student who was also a cripple. A point was reached where Ch'an could no longer take this insult. He told Shen-t'u that from now on he must observe the social conventions that indicate Ch'an's superior status based both on class and physical appearance.

Chia, however, would hear nothing of this. He reminds Ch'an that under their Master's roof, he is the equal of every other student. This situation contrasts with those in the outside world where so-called "normal" people, considering themselves superior to cripples, make fun of people like him. Such ridicule makes him very angry and it is only after being in the presence of the Master that he is able to calm down. There is something about the Master's presence that has a calming influence on others. He reminds Ch'an that he has been cultivating his inner life under the Master for nineteen years and that never once in all those years has the Master paid any attention to Chia's outward appearance. Since both he and the prime minister are "wandering" beyond the limits of the body in their spiritual practices, why does Ch'an insist on bringing their attention back to his physical deficiencies? The prime minister, filled with intense shame, asks Chia not to mention the matter again (Ibid.).

The story of Chia also illustrates what philosopher Karen Warren calls "The Logic of Domination" (in Pojman, 591). This logic proceeds through several stages. The sequence begins with a simple observation that certain qualities that belong to group A do not belong to group B. At stage two, the argument is made that any person that possesses the particular qualities of group A is superior to anyone who lacks these qualities. Stage three concludes that group A is morally superior to group B. In short, the absence of these qualities not only makes group B different but also "inferior." A fourth argument is made that those who are morally superior (possess the superior qualities) have the right to dominate those who are morally inferior. The fifth statement draws the logical conclusion that group A is morally justified in dominating group B (in Pojman, 591-592).

Prime Minister Ch'an was already predisposed to hierarchical thinking. The progression of steps from the observation of the other's difference to the moral right to dominate the other can also be found in the traditional relationship of humans to non-human species, of males to females, of whites to blacks, straights to gays, physically "normal" to the physically abnormal, and, in our context, adults to elders.

In the case of "old people," the characteristics and behaviors that are "different" are judged to be "inferior" to, or inferior versions of, the superior qualities of younger adults. Adults assume the right to define the position of elders as subordinate. This logic is manifest in many ways. One is elder-speak, in which adults speak to elders as if they were small children, using condescending remarks and a patronizing tone of voice. But this bias is even more blatantly visible in the media where they use ageist stereotypes that would be instantly condemned if they were racial in character. Television programs aimed at the large "teeny" population have a field day with demeaning depictions of grandparents and the elderly in general.

The media reminds elders of their subordinate "place" not only through the use of stereotyping but also through just plain neglect. The world of the "consumer" (teenagers, parents, young adults) is considered superior and more real. Of course, this world is also dominant when advertisers and their lackeys push their products. Unfortunately, the result is a world that lacks, due to its media and general social stereotypes, the presence of mature models of humaneness and wisdom. This suggests, in a not-too-subtle way, that there are no such beings. "Isn't this the way things are...or should be?" the consumer of images is subtly asked. Unlike the Master's mirror, which reflects the highest and best possibilities of Chia, this media mirror distorts the image of elders even when it singles them out for the sales pitch.

Chia refused to see himself through the eyes of the two-footed, as if having two feet (or being young) was a personal achievement, but instead turned to his spiritual Master who became a mirror in which to view his hidden wholeness (which was the result of self-cultivation). Chia's appeal to the spiritual unity experienced between him and Ch'an in their great "wandering" and the reflection of this in the non-judgmental mirror of the Master's mind, "opens" the eyes of Ch'an and liberates him. In effect, the Prime Minister experienced a reversal of the logic of domination that had led him to take a dominating stance toward Chia. Ch'an realized that there is a deeper and truer mode of relationship with Chia, one based on their common unity and exemplified by the Master.

He drops his hierarchical thinking based on superficial dualisms of normal/abnormal and aristocrat/commoner.

Eugene Bianchi identifies the unique creativity of elders with a cultivation of their inner resources.

> Creative elders are able to move beyond negative cultural stereotypes of being old by cultivating their inner resources . . . The aesthetic and imaginative dimensions of all the arts are akin to the spiritual because they express the deeper longing of the soul for beauty and meaning . . . Another aspect of cultivating inner resources among creative elders is their ability to cultivate serene self-esteem [and move] from a fear-driven to a love-motivated life. (*The Way*, April 1996, 95)

If members of Adultworld would experience such a transformation in consciousness and values, elders could become mirrors in which adults would glimpse their own deeper potentials and already burgeoning qualities. If elders would begin to develop and to manifest clearly their neglected excellences, adults would look to them for emulation rather than to their teenage children.

IV

What We Reflect Back

Such a wonderful shift in consciousness and sensitivity is an invitation to go deeper. Chapter Five of the *Chuang Tzu* begins with a story about Wang T'ai, a teacher who had his foot cut off as a political punishment.

Uncharacteristically, however, he had attracted as many followers as had Confucius in the state of Lu. Ch'ang Chi asks Confucius about the unusual success of this teacher, especially given his teaching style.

> When he stands up, he doesn't teach, when he sits down
> he doesn't talk things over, yet they go to him empty
> and come away full. Is there indeed a wordless teaching,
> or a heart which is whole though the body is deformed?
> What man is this? (Graham, 76)

Confucius accords the teacher the highest praise, calling him a sage. Confucius' only regret is that he and the rest of humankind haven't flocked to become Wang T'ai's students. But Ch'ang pushes for more insight into this teacher's special talent or unique teaching method. Confucius dives deeper. First, he observes that the teacher's inner state remains calm and unmoved even in the face of external changes, either natural transformations or sudden disasters. As things come and go-- even the "mighty" things such as life and death--his heart/mind (hsin/ xin) is not disturbed or altered. It would remain so, even in the case of a sudden cosmic catastrophe. If Heaven collapsed and Earth fell away, "he would not be lost with them." His mind is aware of the Flawless and his heart "holds fast" to the Ancestor of everything that changes and undergoes transformation. As a result, he is able to relate freely to "the transformations of things" without being attached to them in heart or mind (Graham, 76).

Ch'ang wants to know what Confucius means. Confucius explains that when looked at from the point of view of "differences," there are great distinctions among things. But looked at from the point of view of "sameness," there is a hidden wholeness and unity among the diverse and myriad beings. Looking into "that in which they are one," he observes that this harmony of the whole remains, even as the myriad things change position and as individual things experience loss and gain. Therefore, the teacher considers the loss of his own foot as neither more nor less important in the total scheme of things than any of the other losses to the multitude of other beings at any given moment. His wholeness remains complete despite changes to his physical form. "Looking through" the external changes from within himself, he does not lose his peace. In fact, the crippled teacher's heart goes "roaming in the peace which is from the Power" [de/te] (Graham, 76, 77).

Likewise, elders can learn to broaden their perspective and find their place – and peace — in this incredibly complex, interconnected and ever-flowing universe. Everywhere we look, we observe gain and success, and everywhere we look, we see loss and failure. One being's loss is another's gain. Everywhere is pain and everywhere is pleasure. One being's pain accompanies another being's pleasure. Furthermore, loss and gain, pleasure and pain, succeed one another in the flow: today's experience of success is followed by tomorrow's experience of failure; today's sorrow yields to tomorrow's joy.

Shifting to this broader perspective weans us from the narrow views that are obsessed with differences and where everything that happens to "me" is of ultimate importance and hence the positive or negative value of any being or event is determined accordingly. Chuang Tzu also suggests that we can never know for certain whether what we experience as loss is not, in fact, gain – if not for me, if not now, then maybe for someone else, maybe tomorrow--and what we consider gain is not actually loss – for someone else or for me, maybe now, maybe later. Sometimes it is all of these. If that is so, then one's mental and emotional state, the level of one's self-interest and expectations – all become crucial to determining one's experience and motivating and shaping one's subsequent action.

Paradoxically, letting-go of the assumption that "I" am the reference point for and the key to the meaning of everything, can deepen my sense of identification with all beings, my compassion with their losses and my delight in their joys. My feeling of joy is but one experience of joy among the trillion experiences of joy at any one moment around the world. This fact can make me feel insignificant or it can make me feel connected with and a part of an incredibly rich tapestry of vibrant experiences. My feeling of pain is but one experience among trillions of experiences of pain at any one moment. This can make me feel that my pain is insignificant or it may allow me to feel less alone in the universe and more connected through compassion with the trillion painful experiences occurring right now: some of less, some of more, intensity.

Returning to our story, Confucius' disciple admits that this insight gives the teacher a sense of communion and accommodation with the larger process of which he is a part. He uses his wits to "discover his own heart, his heart to discover the unchanging heart beyond it." Still troubled, Ch'ang Chi states that all of this, as profound as it may be, seems to be simply an individual, private affair. Why does the teacher attract others? Why should all of these people "congregate around him?" (Graham, 77).

Confucius points out that when people want to see their reflections, they do not look into running water but into still water. So, anyone who wants to still his own mind and to experience his or her deep unchanging heart, seeks out the presence of the Master. Confucius alludes to other qualities that may enter into this mysterious attractive power and other metaphors to capture them. He first compares the Master's deeper still mind or heart to the pine or cypress whose secret lies in its extraordinary ability to be rooted in and imbibe the life of Earth and thus to remain green and full of spring (like the unchanging heart) even as the seasons come and go. Like them, the Master remains constant through change but also full of life (Ibid.). (This reminds one of Confucius' teaching on Nag the Hump who carries "constant springtime" in his heart even as he moves through the seasons.)

Confucius also suggests that the Master's influence might be likened to the legendary emperors Yao and Shun who received their endowment from the ordering power of Heaven and hence ordered the empire by simply ordering themselves. Similarly, the Master develops his original endowment (*de/te*) while he deepens his roots in its Source (*Dao/Tao*) and so remains constant, despite outer changes and the passage of time (Graham, 77).

Modern elders who seek wisdom and fullness of mind, heart, and spirit would do well to reflect on what Chuang Tzu's Confucius just said and, when fears strikes, on his claim that, "The test that one holds fast to the Beginning is the fact of not being afraid" (Graham, 77). The Beginning can be found in the present as the ground of one's being and the source of inner individual powers (te/de). "Holding fast" to it makes one much more fearless than even the bravest knight who "will boldly enter a battle of great armies" motivated by ambition to garner fortune and fame. One who "holds fast to the Beginning . . . makes heaven and earth his palace and the myriad things his storehouse. . ." His body is simply a dwelling place and his senses like images or phenomena. Hence, he "treats as one all that wit knows and has a heart which never dies!" (Graham, 77).

Today, instead of looking into still water, we look into mirrors. But this is hardly the same thing. When we look in the mirror and see the development of wrinkles and other signs of aging, what happens? Does the mirror become a screen onto which we project images of a person with smooth skin, full dark hair, perfectly straight and ivory white teeth? But in desiring to look like a twenty-something adult, do we also desire the maturity level of that person? Are we thereby subtly refusing or trivializing the real valuable growth that we have experienced? As James Hillman suggests, a face is a work in progress, an image and "a witness to your character." Character, as Hillman uses the term, resonates with certain qualities of *de*. The late beauty icon Marilyn Monroe made a similar point when she said: "I want to grow old without facelifts. They take the life out of a face, the character. I want to have the courage to be loyal to the face I've made" (Quoted in Thomas, 9).

William Thomas, M.D. imagines a letter written to an advice columnist who expresses pity for Baby Boomers who are unable to develop wrinkles and crows' feet with the result that their skin lacks all character and makes them appear immature. The columnist had encouraged her readers to buy a new cream that changes one's face so that it reflects one's unique individual character like the faces of elders. She is convinced that the obsession with looking young can arrest one's personal and spiritual development.

Reader Looks Older . . . Now Growing Again!

Dear Patty: You've changed my life. I was a "Baby Boomer," obsessed with youth and divorced from my own aging self. When I looked in the mirror, all I saw was flat, featureless skin. I just felt terrible. Then

I read your column about that pharmacist's miracle discovery . . . CF-6 Facial Cream. Well, I bought a jar and amazing things began to happen. It changed my life! I do look older. I'm growing into a wonderful face: wrinkles, crow's feet, smile lines . . . I have it all! I feel great . . . and I'm growing as a person again, thanks to you! (Thomas, 10-11)

WORKS CITED

Graham, A.C. *Chuang Tzu: The Inner Chapters*. Indianapolis: Hackett Publ. Co., 2001.

Mair, Victor H. *Wandering on the Way: Early Taoist Tales and Parables of Chuang Tzu*. New York: Bantam Books, 1994.

Thomas, William H., M.D. *What Are Old People For? How Elders Will Save the World*. Acton, MA: VanderWyk & Burnham, 2004.

Warren, Karen J. "The Power and the Promise of Ecological Feminism." In Louis Pojman and Paul Pojman (eds), *Environmental Ethic: Readings in Theory and Applications*, 6th Edition. Belmont, CA: Thomson Wadsworth (2012) 589-605.

Watson, Burton. *Chuang Tzu: Basic Writings*. New York: Columbia University Press, 1964.

CHAPTER TWO

Childhood to Elderhood

I

Losing our Original Simplicity

Once upon a time an ancient oak tree was cut down in order to carve sacrificial vessels—considered a pious, serious project. Chuang Tzu introduces it and its wider implications as a metaphor for human social conditioning in Chapter Twelve:

> With wood from a hundred-year–old tree
> They made sacrificial vessels,
> Covered with green and yellow designs.

The wood that was cut away
Lies unused in the ditch.
If we compare the sacrificial vessels with the wood in
  the ditch
We find them to differ in appearance:
One is more beautiful than the other
Yet they are equal in this: both have lost their original
  nature.

(Merton, 78)

On the surface these two "products" differ dramatically. But, Chuang Tzu points out that both have lost their original identity and integrity (te/de) and hence their own vital source for continued growth. Similarly, society values the "respectable citizen" and abhors "the criminal". True, a "robber" and a "respectable citizen" are different when judged in terms of their social behavior and reputation. But, as Chuang Tzu states, "they are equal in this: both have lost their original nature" (Ibid).or, their "original simplicity." How has that happened?

Society, according to Chuang Tzu, stimulates desires by attaching value to and promoting certain external objects, types of persons, or appropriate ways of behaving. Society then promises rewards such as personal happiness, social status and wealth, and threatens legal (or illegal) punishment for individuals who take a shortcut (stealing) to acquire its economic "goods." In either case, "Desires unsettle the heart" and increase "Until the original nature runs amok." And, running amok, it chases after scarce goods and honors. Some individuals play by the rules and some do not. But both end up like "prisoners in a cage," even if only one ends up there literally.

Today, educational carpenters and woodworkers are beginning to carve away at the potentials and innate qualities of very young children, deciding which qualities should be developed and "saved" and which should be discarded as were the wood chips. Like an imperial power, Adultworld expands its hold over the "land" not only of childhood but of Elderhood. Its domination over childhood is aided by children's naivete and innocence, their desire to please others and often to avoid punishments if they do not follow the rules of behavior, the courses of study, and finally, the laws laid down by "grown-ups."

When they become "adults" they feel it is their duty or even privilege to use the same type of economic, political, and educational institutions, and their standardized methods to humanize the next generation. Those children who had little encouragement to get in touch with and explore the unique self-creative powers within themselves, see little reason to explore these with and in others since it requires sensitive attention and understanding, activated and developed within the context of "working-with," rather than "working-on."

In his Foreword to Paolo Freire's classic, *Pedagogy of the Oppressed*, Richard Schuall captures the essence of Freire's thoughts on education in these words:

> There is no such thing as a *neutral* educational process. Education either functions as an instrument which is used to facilitate integration of the younger generation into the logic of the present system and bring about conformity or it becomes the practice of freedom, the means by which men and women deal critically and creatively with reality and discover how to participate in the transformation of their world. (Freire, 2003, 34)

And in the spirit of Chuang Tzu, Freire himself states, "What the educator [should do] in teaching is to make it possible for the students to become themselves" (Freire, 1990, 181). Instead many educators are, in effect, telling students that they will control the students' development by determining which abilities and potentials of theirs are to be actualized while ignoring the rest. For Chuang Tzu this is part of losing the original simplicity. Freiere would agree and add: "The more we become able to become a child again, to keep ourselves childlike, the more we can understand that because we love the world and we are open to understanding, to comprehension, that when we kill the child in us, we are no longer" (Freire, 1990, 64). At least we are not a manifestation of our original nature or simplicity. But all is not lost. Elders can recover the child within with its unique potentials (*te/de*) and set out to help others not lose theirs.

Chapter Eighteen of the *Chuang Tzu* contains a parable about the fate of a sea bird that was blown ashore and landed in a sacred precinct.

> The Prince ordered a solemn reception . . .
> Called for musicians
> To play the compositions of Shun,
> Slaughtered cattle to nourish it:
> Dazed with symphonies, the unhappy sea bird
> Died of despair. (Merton, 103)

For Chuang Tzu the message is clear:

> Water is for fish
> And air for men.
> Natures differ, and needs with them.

Hence the wise men of old
Did not lay down
One measure for all. (Merton, 104)

Chuang Tzu's stories about the crippling and sometimes destructive results of treating an individual member of another species as if it were human (thus universalizing human standards and preferences) must be read also as a warning about treating other human beings as if all were basically the same and hence would benefit equally from the same standardized rules of treatment. For Chuang Tzu and most other Taoists, each human has his or her own unique constellation of potentials and his or her own *telde* or inner power for their realization. And as we will see, there are many "ways" that can aid in this growth.

II

Which Child is Normal? Which Abnormal?

The *Lieh Tzu* (*Liezi*) reminds us of how conventional mindsets and judgments reinforce conformity and dissuade people from alternative interpretations of and "ways" to utilize their experiences.

> Mr. P'ang of Ch'in had a son who was clever as a child but suffered from an abnormality when he grew up. When he heard singing he thought it was weeping, when he saw white he thought it was black; fragrant smells he thought noisome, sweet tastes he thought bitter, wrong actions he thought right. Whatever came into his mind...he always turned upside down. (Graham, 72)

It was not that Mr. P'ang did not share in the world of complementary opposites: white/black, fragrant/noisome, sweet/bitter. He simply reversed their qualities. Lieh Tzu asks why it is that abnormal behaviors, attitudes and beliefs are judged negatively, often condemned, and not seen or perhaps appreciated as something "different." For us, they are sometimes labeled too quickly as medical illnesses, psychological disorders, or moral deficiencies.

Mr. P'ang was clever, and, instead of exhausting the family's resources by calling in the usual run of shamans, acupuncturers, and seers, he followed the advice of a Mr. Yang and set out for the state of Lu to seek help from the Confucianists. While passing through the state of Ch'en, however, Mr. P'ang came upon that old Taoist buzzard, Lao Tzu. After hearing Mr. P'ang's story, the Old Master reframed everything, suggesting that it was society that was sick insofar as it suffered from a state of confusion about health and illness, pathology and normality, benefit and harm, right and wrong.

Society's pathology was shared by nearly everyone with the result that no one diagnosed it as a sickness. Why should a family worry if one of its members is abnormal, or a village worry if one of its families is abnormal, or a nation worry if one of its states is abnormal, or the world worry if one of its nations is abnormal? Of course, if the whole world is abnormal, then how could a little normality threaten it? "How do you know your son is abnormal?" the Taoist sage asked. "Supposing the minds of everyone in the world were like your son's, then on the contrary it is you who would be abnormal" (Ibid). In such a world, Lao Tzu is implying, how would the father feel if his family rushed him off to have him cured of the psychological illness of being "different?"

Lao Tzu would say that spending inordinate amounts of time and money in order to produce a diagnostic manual cataloging and categorizing certain mental or physical states as abnormal or deviant is a convenient way for self-appointed guardians of the normal and conventional in a (possibly) abnormal society to prescribe (order) therapies or drugs profiting individuals or corporations already invested heavily in the status quo. It also spares society the unpleasant and difficult task of critically diagnosing its own illness.

Admitting that he himself might be considered a little abnormal, Lao Tzu warns Mr. P'ang about putting too much stock in the advice of "the gentlemen of Lu, who are the most abnormal of all…" Lu, of course, was considered the center of the normal and a model of and for the conventional. Its elite, like Confucius, have the audacity to go around making normative judgments about everyone else. "Who are they," Lao Tzu mocks, "to cure other people's abnormality?" Lao Tzu advises him to go straight home and not to waste his money (Graham, 72-73).

IV

This Teacher of Mine

Creative, imaginative elders, filled with spiritual energy (*shenqi*) and wisdom, could do well as guides for the young. True to their flexible, spontaneous spirit, they would not seek to control their mentees or crank out docile followers. Along these lines, in Chapter Six, Chuang Tzu tells the story of a certain Yi Erh-tzu, a student of Emperor Yao, who went to visit the Taoist recluse Hsu Yu. The recluse had allegedly rejected the offer of Emperor Yao to take over the Empire. Asked what Emperor Yao was teaching him, Yi Erh-tzu summarized it as, "you must learn to practice benevolence and righteousness and to speak clearly about right and wrong!" (Watson, 85).

Hsu Yu was astonished that the student should come to see him, as if his teachings were even slightly similar to those of the (seemingly) Confucian Emperor. Furthermore, "Yao has already tattooed you with benevolence and righteousness, and cut off your nose with right and wrong" (Watson, 85). Hsu Yu draws a parallel between bodily disfigurement inflicted as punishment for political disfavor and the disfiguring of mind and heart by internalizing rigid codes of right and wrong and then regulating one's external behavior so as to comport with them. Given the serious limitations that such a crippled way of life imposes on the mind-heart, how would it be possible for the student to achieve spiritual freedom and hence "to go wandering in any far away, carefree, and as-you-like-it path?" (Watson, 85-6).

The student suggested that his training in morality and the virtues was compatible with at least wandering in "a little corner" of the path (Watson, 86). Hsu Yu rejects that and bluntly tells the emperor's student that the effect of his training is the equivalent of spiritual blindness. Given such a state, it would be impossible for him to *see* the path let alone travel on it. Playing his last card, Yi Erh-tzu draws on historical precedent to argue that, in the past, several famous persons did "forget" and abandoned vain personal qualities such as beauty, strength, and wisdom and thereby experienced transformation. Perhaps "the Creator" would do the same to him, symbolically removing his tattoos and reattaching his nose. While not totally rejecting that possibility, but wanting to drive home his main point, Hsu Yu contrasts *his* "Teacher" and the experience of wandering with him with the narrow ways of righteousness, duty, and virtue provided by and embodied in the Emperor (and incorporated by his student).

> This Teacher of mine, this Teacher of mine--he passes judgment on the ten thousand things but he doesn't think himself righteous; his bounty extends to ten thousand generations but he doesn't think himself long-lived; he covers heaven, bears up the earth, carves and fashions countless forms, but he doesn't think himself skilled. It is with him alone I wander. (Watson, 86)

In the case of Yi Erh-tzu, Hsu Yu doubts whether he can free himself from the damage done to his heart-mind and possibly to his nature. Much of his identity and self-esteem come from comparing himself to others who are judged according to a code of moral absolutes. Given such a limited and limiting self-structure there is little imagination and creative impulse for "wandering in any far away, carefree, and as-you-like-it paths," as the Taoist Master had phrased it (Watson, 86).

An experience of this spiritually subtle level of wandering assumes that one has passed through ever more subtle levels of the body-mind-spirit. We see one articulation of this by Yen Hui when explaining the various facets of "sitting and forgetting." He tells Confucius that he left behind his "limbs and body," his "perception and intellect," his inner "form," and his "understanding," until he made himself "identical with the Great Thoroughfare" (Watson, 87). (Or one might also call it "wandering with" or "wandering" the Great Thoroughfare).

V

The Inner Formless

Zhuangzi insists that humans are not "limited to form [but] can attain to formlessness." They are not "objects" or "resources" to be manipulated and controlled. Because of the Formless, Useless and Creative Spirit, it is always possible to find freedom, despite the legal and sociopolitical pressures to con-form and their promise of owning more, having more control over "things" and thus gain power. However, for Chuang Tzu, one's "law" should be within one's self. That way one "walks in hiddenness" and one's actions are not dictated from the outside. If one's "law" comes from the outside, then one will seek "to extend his power" over objects or things to gain security. The problem is, "those objects gain control over him" (Merton, 136).

The motivation behind much standardization is a desire to wield power over others by controlling all aspects of their lives through the use of laws, rules, standard operating procedures, etc. Part of this is made easier by a child's desire to please others, especially adults. As a reward for internalizing these external controls, and shaping one's identity accordingly, one is given some power of one's own. Seeking more power over "objects" (sometimes people), one plays a role assigned to him in the social drama and receives appropriate applause. Unlike the spirit-rich person, this individual's acts are strongly motivated and dictated by the approval and disapproval of others and institutions. Lacking contact with the creative, guiding, and nurturing power within, one's acts are not self-rewarded experiences. Nor can one acknowledge that such a power might exist within others and therefore demands of us that we "let-be" and sensitively support, not shape and control the other.

A wise elder might choose to help a child explore and develop his or her own innate qualities which are of intrinsic value, saying, "Regardless of how the representatives of the educational or commercial systems judge your performance and hand out their symbols of extrinsic value (grades, salaries, etc.), in this family we affirm and celebrate your unique personal qualities and abilities. Continue to develop them, even if society, no, especially if society, thinks of them as useless." Such a speech, of course, can only come from grandparents or other elders who are developing their own inner riches and, secure in themselves, are willing to spend time with a child, to listen to him or her, and to help nourish the personal riches with which the child is graced, or, en-daoed.

Elders must play this important role when the gale winds of educational fashion, indoctrination and coercion blow strongly against the blossoming petals of the individual child's spirit. Elders can often see more clearly what needs to be done for children than harried parents who sometimes reluctantly, sometimes in relief, turn over the job of making their children "useful" to the educational, commercial and entertainment "industries." Many parents themselves have naively adopted Adulthood's valuation of "usefulness" as their own standard by which to judge both elders and children.

Elders who begin to see this connection will feel increasingly moved to help children. Unfortunately, they will find that interlocked social structures work to keep elders from alliances-in-uselessness with children. Elders who want to free children from the carving knives of the purveyors of usefulness, must also work to free themselves from a complex of internal and external forces working against their own liberation. They will see that children at a very early age are being trained to be anxious about their futures. Parents and educators mouth Adultworld shibboleths about "getting into the college of your (our) choice" and/or training well for "the increasingly competitive global economy." Once this anxiety is created by Adultworld, its evangelists promise to lift the burden of sin if the children will behave themselves and comply with the dictums handed down from on high.

VI

Children and Animals: Opening the Mind-Heart To The "Other"

We inflict great pain when we divide the earth into the human and non-human, cling to the human and wage war on the non-human. We inflict pain when we force other life forms to serve our interests: economic, social and even religious. Especially regarding the latter, we can do so with the best of intentions.

We saw this with the Seabird that flew ashore and was so inundated with human cultural expressions that it died.

There is a more individual case in the tale from Chapter Nineteen of the *Chuang Tzu*. The Grand Augur (priest/invocator/diviner of the Ancestors) tells the swine who are destined to die in a sacrificial ritual that they should feel happy because they have been blessed with a nobler existence than have other pigs. Because of their special status and destiny they are to be given the best in food, drink, and living conditions. However, in an unguarded moment, the Grand Augur looks at this situation through the eyes of the swine. He wonders if perhaps they would prefer to have fewer honors and more years to live. Quickly, however, he dismisses such a radical thought, and reiterates the religious principle that the swine have been chosen for a higher, nobler type of existence. In fact, Chuang Tzu has the Augur recognizing that perhaps he understands the swine's position because it resembles his own. For while he is honored with title and position, it is very likely that his own career, if not his very life, will be shortened given the volatile nature of the politics of the time. Ironically, this realization only reinforces his decision not to let swine off the hook that hoisted his own petards.

> So he decided against the pigs' point of view, and adopted his own point of view, both for himself and for the pigs also. How fortunate those swine, whose existence was thus ennobled by one who was at once an officer of the state and a minister of religion. [xix. 6] (Merton, 108)

Every year billions of "dumb" animals are sacrificed for the taste and comfort of "rational" animals. True rationality, however, demands that we "bracket" our human-centered prejudices and biases, just as bracketing our self-centered standpoint in order to consider the effects of our actions on other humans is a rational and moral thing to do. Would we not want others to reciprocate? Factory farming, whose aim is the most efficient and profitable production of food, causes tremendous pain both directly or indirectly.

The pain suffered by individuals because of factory style education or the cramming of them together in chicken coops called nursing homes are benignly overlooked by Adultworld. Undoubtedly, the authority carried by manuals written by "experts" in life-span development, like the authority of manuals written by "agricultural" experts, provide both scientific support and a vocabulary that misnames and justifies the pain as it teaches deference to the authority of the mediators and purveyors of scientific, sociological, political, etc. and faith in their alleged truths. One way to deconstruct the dominant narrative justifying factory farming, factory schooling, etc. is to develop a sensitivity to the inner life and unique value of the "other" undergoing allegedly beneficial treatment in accordance with the general social-scientific narrative that outlines the justification for it. Then uncover their narrative of domination, which, in the case of children, means listening to their stories.

The Grand Augur found the act of taking the point of view of another to be unnerving, not only because it raised the possibility of a fully legitimate if alternative narrative to his own, but also because of the light it shed on his own condition. Likewise with schools: despite the rhetoric about educating for citizenry in a democratic society with its values of individual freedom, independent thinking, etc., its actual rewards and incentives are for conformity, "mastery" of packaged material, enforced work, group think (exams, grades), obedience to institutionally appointed superiors, etc. Teachers, supervisors and administrators in State-run schools pass along to students the same values that they themselves have internalized and that are expressed through exercising their own roles and eliminating their own critical voices. They also become agents for the larger corporate run economic system who, wringing their hands, wait to select the best "products" produced by factory schooling. The personal/behavioral as well as the content/skilled lessons learned are now further reinforced and rewarded financially. No wonder elders who want to move in the direction of mental and spiritual freedom, of imaginative "wandering," have to go through a real struggle with internalized self-judgments, slavish loyalties, and addictive behaviors surrounding consumerism and the work ethic.

Chuang Tzu encouraged humans to use their minds and hearts to adopt the point of view of other humans and other living beings. This would certainly be a radically different starting point for a philosophy of nature than the one built on an assumed preeminence of the human point of view. Compare the attitude found in the previous two stories with one found in Chapter One. This is the famous incident where Chuang Tzu dreamt he was a butterfly. He felt and moved as a butterfly, not thinking himself as a human dreaming he was a butterfly. When he woke up, he was Chuang Tzu. The Question: was he Chuang Tzu dreaming he was a butterfly or is he now a butterfly dreaming he is Chuang Tzu?

Chuang Tzu believed deeply in the immanent power of the Tao to bring freedom. He did not divide reality into a deterministic realm called "nature" or "body" and a transcendent free realm called "spirit" or "mind." Rather, he held that the natural, the social, and the personal "ways" were capable of an integrated holistic Way guided by Tao. Usually, it was the deterministic mechanism of the social machine that threatened personal freedom and interrupted the flow of Tao, not nature. By reducing personhood to individual ego, society made true wisdom and creativity difficult. Nature, for Taoists, was not the model of uncivilized chaos, the reign of the "law of the jungle," as it was for conservative Confucianists like Hsun Tzu. Rather, it was a harmonious and spontaneously functioning whole. Chuang Tzu seemed to believe that the "violence" of nature, usually short-lived and contained, was nothing compared to the physical violence of humans towards natural beings and their psychological violence towards other humans, some of it is subtle like the forced shaping of minds and hearts of persons to physical violence wrought individually or through wars and state-enforced slavery.

WORKS CITED

Freire, Paulo. *Pedagogy of the Oppressed*. New York: Continuum, 2003.

Freire, Paolo and Myles Horton. *We Make the Road by Walking: Conversations on Education and Social Change*. Philadelphia: Temple University Press, 1990.

Graham, A.C., *The Book of Lieh-Tzu*. New York: Columbia University Press, 1990.

Merton, Thomas. *The Way of Chuang Tzu*. New York: New Directions Publishing Corp., 1965.

Watson, Burton, tr. *Chuang Tzu: Basic Writings*. New York: Columbia University Press, 1964.

CHAPTER THREE

FORgetting

You've heard of forgetting the remembered;
Have you heard of forgetting the forgotten?
Chuang Tzu/Zhuangzi, paraphrase

"To forget things and to forget heaven is called forgetting the self. The man who forgets himself is said to have entered heaven" (C.T.12, Mair, 109)

I

You'd Forget Your Head

Who hasn't, as they've grown older, been criticized by others or themselves about "forgetting"? You forget your keys, you forget birthdays, you forget names and dates—"you'd forget your head if it wasn't attached," your spouse remarks, only half in jest. Obviously, people with Post Traumatic Stress Syndrome wish they could forget. That is an extreme and deeply unfortunate condition. And, for many of us, there are memories of events and people we all wish we could forget. Psychologists tell us that memories are stored selectively, that some are seriously flawed, that many are reedited and only partially resemble the actual event. There are short-term memories and long-term memories. Some people are better at recalling one kind than the other; some lose one kind more than the other. And there are people with photographic memories whose brains are loaded with images of pages, musical scores, etc.

And yet, recent research has begun questioning the totally negative, declinist interpretation of memory loss in the older brain. Forgetting is not, in many cases, a purposeless, unavoidable affliction, but rather a technique used by the older brain to aid in its search for deeper patterns and connections. It is a strategy for ignoring what is irrelevant in a mass of data or a situation. This wider attention span may help elders grasp the relevance of data and the deeper message from a situation than can the mind of younger individuals. This ability may be what we have in mind when we think of older people as wise. Indeed, research on wisdom being conducted at the University of Michigan confirms recent research on memory. According to Dr. Jacqui Smith: "If older people are taking in more information from a situation, and they're then able to combine it with their comparatively greater store of general knowledge, they're going to have a nice advantage." (NY Times "Older Brain Really May Be a Wiser Brain" 5/20/08)

The current hysteria over "forgetfulness" not only turns the normal into the abnormal and pathological, but, as Margaret M. Gullette, a scholar at the Women's Studies Research Center at Brandeis University has argued, it can turn mentally and emotionally healthy individuals into anxious, guilt-ridden ones, some of whom commit suicide rather than face a future ruled by dementia. Her 2011 University of Chicago book, *Fighting the New Ageism in America* is a classic in the field. In her New York Times Op-Ed piece, "Our Irrational Fear of Forgetting," Gullette points out:

> Most forgetfulness is not Alzeihmer's, or dementia, or even necessarily a sign of cognitive impairment. And yet any prophecy about impaired cognition—whether it is fulfilled or not—harms people's sense of self. They begin to be treated like children, patronized with baby talk or avoided . . . The mind is capacious. Much mental and emotional ability can survive mere memory loss, as do other qualities that make us human. (*New York Times*, pg. WK9, May 22, 2011)

Gullette is optimistic, suggesting that an increasing number of people are "aware of alternative narratives of memory loss." She admires the saying, "Forget Memory, Try Imagination" (Ibid). Whatever the case, elders should be skeptical of both their well-meaning relatives and conventionally trained counselors who reduce the meaning of their experiences to signs of inevitable declining mental powers and preach the art of resignation or prescribe an arsenal of medications.

In *Spirituality and Aging*, Robert C. Atchley demonstrates that although memory, especially short-term memory, may diminish in the early stages of dementia, long term memory endures and allows for a sense of continuity with the past, including one's spiritual experiences. Even in the advanced stages of dementia, where people can lose distant memories, "they still have a strong connection with the present" (Atchley, 42). And these people "still exhibit many of the traits we prize most in personhood" (Ibid.). Atchley refers to one of Frances Hellebrandt's portraits of people in a dementia ward where she had made observations over a number of years:

> They move about freely, often in pairs, showing evidence of concern for one another even though they never address each other by name and cannot identify the person with whom they are walking . . . The casual observer would find the group deceptively normal. . . . None knows their behavior is in any way aberrant. Neither do they realize they live in an institution. Yet much of what we consider positive human qualities remain alive in these people – concern for others, friendliness, optimism. (in Atchley, 42)

Atchley argues that if one accepts the definition of basic spirituality as beingness, then "as long as there is being there is the possibility of spirituality, and as long as there is spirituality, there is a right to be considered a person. In fact, the experience of beingness may be the last experience to be lost in dementia" (Atchley, 42). And many of the higher or deeper states of "Being" toward which "forgetting" and other practices point, can transform many aspects of one's own being.

Early Daoists like Chuang Tzu provide what Gullette calls "alternative narratives" wherein "forgetting" becomes part of a process that frees one to launch into ever-more subtle states of being and consciousness as well as take on a practice or way (*tao/dao*) that leads to a richer yet more flexible integration of body, mind, spirit. Elders (or older adults) need not shudder with fear at the experience of forgetting. There are other "ways" to interpret and even develop it.

Interestingly, most contemplative paths, East and West, lead one through a process of "forgetting" in one form or another as a means to the discovery and unfolding of a deeper personal/spiritual life that is also a grounding in a more universally encompassing Whole. Such high states of awareness, while transforming and even moving beyond the usual mind-body experience, also, when the time is ripe, allow one to reenter and focus on the world with new intensity and awe. A person may still experience what is commonly understood as "forgetting," but the positive contemplative practice that begins with but radically expands the possibilities and intensifies the effects of "forgetting," can take one into extremely subtle levels of knowing and being where one ultimately "forgets forgetting."

Ii

Forgetting Can Awaken Other Possibilities

As usual, ancient Taoists/Daoists like Chuang Tzu/Zhuangzi and the later Lieh Tzu/Liezi enjoyed poking fun at and shaking confidence in the commonly held beliefs concerning forgetting and memory loss, among many others. We start as always with a story, this time one by Lieh Tzu/Liezi in the work named after him.

The *Lieh Tzu* tells a tale about Hua-Tzu, a middle-aged man who had lost his memory. As it describes Hua's condition:

> He would receive a present in the morning and forget it by the evening, give a present in the evening and forget it by the morning. In the street he would forget to walk, at home he would forget to sit down. Today he would not remember yesterday, tomorrow he would not remember today. (Graham, 70)

Experts from all of the medical, religious, and moral institutions of the time were called upon to "cure" this man. A shaman, a diviner, and finally a doctor were called in and each did their best but to no avail. At last (and much to the rhetorical delight of Taoists), a Confucian therapist from the state of Lu was consulted. Of course, it cost the family half of its property to pay for his services. The Confucianist confirmed the obvious by announcing that none of these other arts and sciences had worked on this man, but declared, "I shall try reforming his mind, changing his thoughts; there is a good chance that he will recover" (Graham, 71).

After testing the man's responsiveness and satisfying himself that the man could be cured, he ordered everyone out of the man's room because his arts were a family secret (obviously he had skills not taught by Confucius). And, lo! the malady that had plagued the man for years was lifted within a single morning. But—and here is Taoist irony--when the patient woke up, he was very angry. "He dismissed his wife, punished his sons, and chased away the Confucian with a spear" (Ibid.). The police placed the man under arrest for his disgraceful treatment of a Confucian scholar from Lu (Ibid.). But why was the man so upset? Why didn't he appreciate this return to "normality"? What had been so valuable about his full-blown state of forgetfulness?

Hua-tzu knew that he could not expect a Confucianist, a defender and promoter of the conventional view, to understand. "Formerly, when I forgot," said Hua-Tzu, "I was boundless; I did not notice whether heaven and earth existed or not." Hua-tzu used his spells of forgetting as a way to simplify and clear his mind, expand his consciousness and widen his horizons. He was also angry at this sudden regaining of memory because with it "all the disasters and recoveries, gains and losses, joys and sorrows, loves and hates of twenty or thirty years past rise up in a thousand tangled threads." He now fears that his mind is ruined and that when new pains and joys, gains and losses occur, his mind and heart will "be confounded." He wistfully asks, "Shall I never again find a moment of forgetfulness?" (Graham, 71).

Ironically, Tzu Kung, Confucius' model student, presented this perplexing story of Hua Tzu to his Master. Confucius responded, "This is beyond the understanding of someone like you." Confucius then told his secretary to make a record of these events (Graham, 72).

According to our conventional wisdom, elders who find themselves forgetting names or conversations or who search for words that are "on the tip of their tongues" should feel badly. Yet, Hua Tzu rejoiced in "forgetting" and embraced the possibilities it offered to approach life in an open, holistic way. His story suggests that memory loss or forgetfulness might serve as a "calling" or a signal to explore new states of consciousness and modes of awareness—a crazy wisdom.

The *Zhuangzi*, according to Philip J. Ivanhoe, can be seen as therapeutic in nature: "a kind of medicine aimed at relieving a particular kind of malady" (Ivanhoe, 90). Developing the art of "forgetting" can serve elders in a special way by helping them abandon corrupting "knowledge" and return "to an earlier, more innocent mode of being" (Ivanhoe, 90). Through "forgetting," as Ivanhoe points out, we lighten the heavy influence that education and socialization have over the mind-heart (*xin*), and hence over what we may or may not do. We practice "forgetting" to free ourselves from constricting internalized directives, "in order to allow the spontaneous movements of the Dao to inform and guide us" (Ivanhoe, 98). Instead of the traditional emphasis on learning and *"making up* our minds to follow Confucianism, Zhuangzi urges us to *unmake* our minds and unify our intentions by following the Dao," notes Ivanhoe (Ibid.). "Forgetting" *(wang)* as a general theme in the *Zhuangzi*, emphasizes "the need to abandon" and to eliminate "misguided and harmful distinctions society has inculcated in us from the beginning . . . and work to eliminate the various artificial categories and unnatural orientations that warp our perceptions and judgments"(Ivanhoe, 99). Forgetting, by eliminating their influence, helps to create space within us for "Dao to gather and guide us," says Ivanhoe, paraphrasing *Zhuangzi* (Ibid.).

Hence, it is possible for an elder to move on from rudimentary experiences of "forgetting" to develop a wider mental context wherein the "spontaneous" acts of "forgetting" are not only welcomed, but where the practice of forgetting becomes part of a "way" (*Tao*) leading to a fuller transformation. Thereby an elder will be able to dismiss the conventional negative judgments that interpret acts of "forgetting" as signs of mental decline associated with aging. Rather, they can be considered an invitation to explore a mode of consciousness available to elders who are ready to grow personally and spiritually beyond their adult phase. Unfortunately, there are few counselors or spiritual directors capable of facilitating elders in this search.

III

Sitting and Forgetting (zuo wang)

In Chapter Six of the *Chuang Tzu/Zhuangzi*, Confucius instructs one of his disciples in the "way" of forgetting. Eventually the disciple goes beyond anything Confucius had experienced and hence was asked by his teacher to teach him (or counsel the counselor). Through the practice known as "sitting and forgetting," Yen Hui, a student of Confucius, was able to attain higher levels and richer modes of consciousness and being.

As he improved, this enthusiastic neophyte would appear before his Master and proudly announce, "I'm improving!" (Watson, 86). Confucius would then ask him to explain. The first time, Yen Hui said that he had "forgotten" the Confucian virtues of benevolence *(jen/ren)* and righteousness *(yi/i)*. Chuang Tzu's Taoist-like Confucius approved of this, but only as a first step. His challenge, "you still haven't got it" encouraged his disciple to continue (Watson, 87). Yen Hui went away to practice more forgetting. Some time later, he returned to his Master and again declared, "I'm improving!" Asked to elaborate, he proudly explained that he had now forgotten "rites and music" which implied that he had now "forgotten" much of the basic Confucian tradition (Ibid.). But Confucius was still not satisfied.

After some time has passed, Yen Hui reported back, again announcing that he was improving. Asked to explain, the disciple says, "I can sit down and forget everything!" (Ibid.). Confucius was "startled" by this statement and anxiously sought a fuller explanation. Yen Hui said that at this level of forgetting he had dropped off his trunk and limbs, driven away sensations and perceptions, cast away his physical form, eliminated understanding, and made himself identical with the Great Transformational Way. Confucius said that if he was "identical with it," he would no longer have preferences or likes; if he had been transformed, he would no longer have norms or constants. Humbling himself before his student, Confucius called Yen Hui "a worthy man" and asked to be taught *by him*! (Watson, 87).

Similarly, for the sagely elder to emerge, he or she will have to work at "forgetting" much of their adult self with its complex web of attachments to everything from social codes to personal preferences as well as to intrusive memories with their respective confining modes of thought and behavior. The creative potentials *(te/de)* of the elder would be freed to be more fully expressive and engaged. "Forgetting" is an individual path of letting-go and letting-be that also allows one to become aware of, open to, and aligned with, the wider as well as the inner transformative energies of the Way.

In short, "forgetting" becomes part of a "way" to the transformation of knowing, doing, and, indeed, being. As one returns to daily life, one perceives and experiences it differently. One is increasingly sensitized to the Whole and how each being's inner depth is rooted in and dynamically united to other beings through and in the Whole. Thus having emptied one's self, let-go of and "forgotten" the bonds of mental and emotional attachments, one is ready to allow the Way to gather within one's deeper self and lead one to a flowing union with All. One "sees" or "experiences" other beings (including natural beings) for what they really are individually as well as in their mutual and harmonious interrelations. One is able to let them be and to act in a way that is consistent with and that participates in the nourishing and guiding energies of the Way.

IV

Forgetting and the Fasting of the Mind-Heart (hsin/xin)

Forgetting as a practice was also linked to a discipline that Zhuangzi's Confucius calls "fasting of the mind/heart" (*hsin/xin*). In Chapter Four of the *Zhuangzi,* Confucius is heard advising his disciple Yen Hui on how to prepare for a meeting with a ruler. During a lengthy discussion, Confucius paradoxically warns that applying all of the abilities that he has grasped through his Confucian education and all of the modes of behavior that he had learned might well prove disastrous. Confucius tells the dazed student that he must fast. Yen Hui says that his family is poor and so he hasn't had meat or wine in a long time. Could that be considered fasting?

Confucius points out that the kind of fasting Yen Hui is alluding to is similar to the one done prior to religious sacrifices. Rather, *he* is talking about fasting of the mind or mind/heart. Yen Hui asks for further instruction. Confucius points out that the key to this kind of fasting is to "unify your attention" (Graham, 68), or "merge all of your intentions into a singularity" (Ziporyn, 26), or achieve an "inner unity" (Merton, 52). You must learn to *listen* and *hear,* but not with your bodily ears as such or with the intellectual understanding based in your mind but with your "spirit, with your whole being" (Merton, 52). The ears can only listen to and hear external sounds. The understanding of the mind is limited to words, labels, and calculations derived from sense experience. But since the *ch'i/qi* (vital energy, primal breath or "spirit") does not listen to particular objects or sounds, whether sensual or mental, such a type of listening, claims Confucius, "demands the emptiness of all the faculties." When this state of emptiness is reached, "then the whole being listens" (Merton, 52-53). As Watson translates it:

> Confucius said, 'Make your will one! Don't listen with your ears, listen with your mind. No, don't listen with your mind, but listen with your spirit. Listening stops with your ears, the mind stops with recognition, but spirit is empty and waits on all things. The Way gathers in emptiness alone. Emptiness is the fasting of the mind.' (Watson, 54)

For Confucius, this mode of holistic listening or attention amounts to "a direct grasp" with your whole being "of what is right there before you that can never be heard with the ear or understood with the mind." As you empty your faculties, they (you) are freed from limitation and preoccupation. What emerges is a state of "unity and freedom" (Merton, 53).

The general movement of one's being towards a higher unity and freedom, as explained here in the *Zhuangzi*, is similar to that found in the *Lieh-Tzu/ Liezi*:

> I can look and listen without the use of my ears and eyes . . . My body merges with my mind; my mind merges with my vital energy (*qi*), my vital energy merges with my spirit, and my spirit merges with nothingness (emptiness) (wu). (tr. Rur-Bin Yang, in Cook, 96)

Yen Hui suddenly understands! He realizes that: "'What was standing in my way was my own self-awareness. If I can begin this fasting of the heart, self-awareness will vanish. Then I will be free from limitation and preoccupation! Is that what you mean?'" Confucius answers affirmatively and through a striking analogy connects this fasting with Yen Hui's previous desire to influence the ruler and others in a positive way. "'Look at this window: it is nothing but a hole in the wall, but because of it the whole room is full of light. So when the faculties are empty, the heart is full of light. Being full of light it becomes an influence by which others are secretly transformed'" (Merton, 53). Such a transformation will enable him to be sensitive to and deal with the king and the changing circumstances that he will face at the court. If after he has emptied his mind or "forgotten" all ambition, he approaches the ruler and the ruler accepts him, at that point he will be ready to teach the ruler.

Confucius counsels him to value stillness, to turn his ears and eyes inward toward a deeper listening and "seeing" that goes beyond the conceptualizing, calculating level of the mind to an inner deeper level where he merges with the Power-that-transforms *(Dao)*. Through letting-go of negative mental and emotional states--a kind of "forgetting"--one can then develop an open, receptive and responsive state of mind where one's *ch'i/qi* "'vital energies' are not committed to or directed by any particular, personal purpose," claims Philip Ivanhoe. Rather, in this state of "vital receptivity" to Dao's gathering, one becomes sensitive to the patterns of its movement within and without, able now to join and flow with them (Ivanhoe, 99-100).

Some elders might appreciate the Zen-like quality of Confucius' crazy wisdom. The Master states:

> It is easy to stand still and leave no trace, but it is hard to walk without touching the ground . . . You know that one can fly with wings: you have not yet learned about flying without wings. You are familiar with the wisdom of those who know, but you have not yet learned the wisdom of those who know not. (Merton, 53)

One would hope that elders, "forgetting" accretions and being "empty" of self-aggrandizing motives and actions, could develop a deeper and wider sensitivity to and experience of the world of Nature and Humanity (a state of unity and freedom). Thus an elder would be able to function as a source of vital/spiritual nourishment for others and a channel through which the wider creative process that subtly transforms the world, not in accord with the dreams of profiteers or ideologues, but in accord with the Way.

As we shall see, there are other "ways" (*taos/daos*) that involve the whole person, integrating all levels within one higher harmony of knowing, being, doing. Some might involve a sensitive, responsive, total presence to and penetrating perception of other beings. Others might focus on one of the movement arts, like *t'ai chi chuan/*

taijiquan, that casts "remembering" in a whole new light and where "forgetting" is forgotten, since all levels of the person take over together and enact the learned movements and ways of perceiving. Many of these would be perfect for elders seeking renewal through new ways of being/ doing.

DONALD P. ST. JOHN

WORKS CITED

Atchley, Robert C. *Spirituality and Aging*. Baltimore: Johns Hopkins University Press, 2009.

Graham, A.C. *Chuang Tzu: The Inner Chapters*. Second Edition Indianapolis, IN: Hackett Publishing Company, 2001

Graham, A.C., *The Book of Lieh-Tzu*. New York: Columbia University Press, 1990.

Gullette, Margaret M. *Agewise: Fighting the New Ageism in America*. Chicago: The University of Chicago Press, 2011.

Gullette, Margaret M. "Our Irrational Fear of Forgetting," *New York Times: The Opinion Pages* May 21, 2011.

Hellebrandt, Frances. "The Senile Dement in our Midst," *Gerontologist* 18:67-70.

Ivanhoe, Philip J. and Karen Leslie Carr. *The Sense of Antirationalism: The Religious Thought of Zhuangzi and Kierkegaard*. Create Space Independent Publishing Platform, 2010.

Jullien, Francois. *Vital Nourishment: Departing from Happiness*. Zone Books, 2007.

Merton, Thomas. *The Way of Chuang Tzu*. New York: New Directions Publishing Corp., 1965.

Reistad-Long, Sara. "Older Brain Really May be a Wiser Brain," *New York Times:* Research Section, May 20, 2008.

Watson, Burton, tr. *Chuang Tzu: Basic Writings*. New York: Columbia University Press, 1964, 1996.

Yang, Rur-Bin. "From 'Merging the Body with the Mind' to 'Wandering in Unitary *Qi*': A Discussion of Zhuangzi's Realm of True Man an its Corporeal Basis. In *Hiding the World in the World*, ed., Scott Cook. Albany: SUNY Press, 2003, pp. 88-127.

Ziporyn, Brook, "How Many Are the Ten Thousand Things and I?" in Scott Cook, editor. *Hiding the World in the World: Uneven Discourses on the Zhuangzi* (Suny Series in Chinese Philosophy and Culture) Albany: SUNY Press (2003) 33-63.

CHAPTER FOUR

Wandering

I

The Urge to Wander

In popular discourse about elders, "wandering" is often associated with forgetting, as in, "she forgot where she was going and just wandered around." Even more directly, the same medical condition that causes increased forgetfulness is often blamed for an elder's desire to "wander." Both are departures from what passes for mental and social normality. Alzheimer's, in some cases, increases the urge to "wander." This could be dangerous and so on one level needs to be observed and curtailed. However...

One typical interpretation of "wandering" appears when a supervisor of a Nursing Home sternly questions an occupant: "Were you out wandering around again? Did you forget where you were? Do we have to lock you up?" Within the context of popular modern culture, forgetting and wandering are interconnected in a negative way. Chuang Tzu also connects them, but within a positive context. For him, and other contemplatives, the practice of "forgetting" eventually frees the mind/heart (*xin/hsin*) from the social (and often internalized personal) shackles that keep one from responding fully to the urge to explore a higher freedom, consciousness and state of being—one experienced during wandering (sometimes while still seated). The desire to wander can be seen as an expression of a deep cosmic unrest exacerbated by the narrow conventional parameters imposed on elders: biological, psychological, and social. In addition, their spirits are increasingly frustrated by the lack of spontaneous moments of genuine joy. In their place are low level chuckles that come from staged games and play.

Trained in conventional thinking, most family members laugh at and criticize a grandparent or other elder for "wandering." Wandering is defined as simply forgetting where one is going. How often is a well-meaning grandchild heard to say, "There is grandpa out back again, just wandering around, lost." Lost? To spontaneously wander in a free and purposeless way is not necessarily to be lost. Being lost assumes one is confused about the way to an intended goal. For Chuang Tzu, the goal of wandering is simply wandering--there is no destination that is being lost sight of or "forgotten." On the other hand, to "get somewhere," whether in terms of a career, marriage or political power, is an imperative controlling much of the behavior of adults. The "crazy" elder deliberately forgets about getting anywhere in particular so that he or she might be free to go No-where and wander in the land of "Nothing Whatsoever."

Our culture is pretty oblivious to the patterns and meanings of mental states and actions based in contemplative and sometimes mystical traditions, such as those reflected in the *Chuang Tzu/ Zhuangzi*. Many of these traditions consider "forgetting" and "wandering" to be means by which one can gain access to, explore, and develop higher states of freedom, play, and imaginative creativity.

To give further insight into the fuller meaning of "wandering," Chuang Tzu uses similes such as "drifting," "rambling," and "meandering." He states: "Aimless wandering does not know what it seeks; demented drifting does not know where it goes" (tr. Watson, 1968,121-122, quoted by Mair in "Wandering," 108). "Demented drifting" is a colorful-even startling-modern correlate to "aimless wandering." As Burton Watson notes, "Chuang Tzu employs the metaphor of a totally free and purposeless journey, using the word *yu* (to wander, or wandering) to designate the way in which the enlightened man wanders through all of creation, enjoying its delights without ever becoming attached to any one part of it" (Watson, 1996, 6). Thus, to happily flow with the flux of existence implies wandering beyond selfish attachment to things. It also suggests being free of those conventional and often internalized expectations that keep an elder's movements under control and only allow him or her the freedom to travel along approved, well-marked and charted paths (literally and figuratively).

But, as Zhuangzi states: "If you have the capacity to wander, how can you keep from wandering?" (Watson,137). And, as Victor H. Mair writes, "If you are incapable of wandering but have the desire to learn, then there is no better place to start than with the practice of 'forgetting'." Forgetting elicits a type of freedom that, in its carefree mode, suggests leaving things behind and moving with the new breezes (Mair, "Wandering," 112-113). This freedom, this leaving things behind, and this moving with new breezes strongly suggest entrance into a new stage in life. Or in the words of Joan Chittister, "we strip ourselves of whatever it is we have accrued until this time in order to give ourselves wholly to the birthing of the person within. Into this part of life we travel light . . . *A blessing of these years is the invitation to go lightfooted into the here and now*" (Chittister, 91).

One who wanders knows freedom as well as joy. For Chuang Tzu, says Mair, "Wandering is a way based on the Way. . . [a way] to exist harmoniously in one's element" ("Wandering," 113). In its broadest expanse, one's element is the universe and so "to be in harmony with the universe is to experience joy" (Ibid).

The elder wanderer's mind is peaceful, playful, and unattached—like that of the pre-adult child but on a post-adult level. He or she has eliminated ("forgotten") many of our utilitarian society's exhortations to prove our worth by "getting somewhere." Unfortunately, many elders have never experienced the joy of wandering: mentally, spiritually or geographically. They have decided to be "stagnantly sedentary" and "to adopt a stance that resists the natural flow of change and hence to fall out of harmony with the universe" (Ibid). "[W]andering in a care-free manner" is antithetical to the modern notion of traveling a road or highway with a well-defined destination and purpose. Mair emphasizes that for Chuang Tzu, "wandering by its very nature is without design . . . [t]he wanderer requires no signposts and has no destination. The sole purpose of his *wandering* is *wandering* itself" (Mair, "Wandering," 108).

As suggested earlier, Chuang Tzu associates wandering *(yu)* with "play," "playing around," and with a free-floating "creative imagining." Wandering, therefore, does not always indicate physical movement. Indeed, the "heavenly wandering" of the heart-mind *(xin)* is experienced when the body is at rest and the mind/heart has reached a high state of consciousness. Forgetting and leaving-behind the influence of sense data, mental conceptualizations, and moral rules, one wanders with Heaven and Earth and is able to "Embody to the fullest what has no end and wander where there is no trail" (Watson tr., in Mair "Wandering," 108).

Elders should take note of the words of Cloud General found in Chapter Eleven of the *Chuang Tzu*: "Nourish your mind./Merely situate yourself in nonaction,/And things will evolve of themselves . . .Forget all relationships and things; /Join in the great commonality of boundlessness" (Mair, 99). In terms of being an elder, one should release one's mind, free one's spirit and, being empty, watch the 10,000 things emerge and then return to their roots, each doing so without being aware of it (Ibid.). Having no rigid self, we can be friends with Heaven and Earth, perhaps even wandering with the Creator in the *yiqi* (unitary energy or single breath) of Heaven and Earth. The designation "wandering elder," then, suggests a person exploring higher forms of spiritual freedom and joy, and not the more stagnant and sedentary prisoner locked in by what Blake saw as the industrial world's "mind-forged manacles."

II

Wandering, Playing, Roaming

We should also be aware of those other "highly vivid verbal images that Chuang-tzu points to as connected with wandering such as dawdling, drifting, floating, rambling, strolling, gawking, sauntering, flowing, trickling, roaming, riding, coming and going, viewing the sights, roving and dillydallying (Mair, "Wandering," 107). In terms of the mental and ultimately spiritual type of wandering, "forgetting" becomes central as "the process whereby the heart-mind is made sufficiently clean and clear that it may engage in *wandering*" (Mair, "Wandering," 109). For those who have "forgotten" self and its complex of social identities, wandering becomes "a technical term for that transcendental sort of free movement which is the mark of an enlightened being" (Mair, "Wandering," 385).

In Chapter Six of the *Chuang Tzu*, three friends ask each other questions, including "Who can climb up to heaven, and wander in the mists, roam the infinite, and forget life forever and forever?" (Watson, 1996, 82). This echoes Hua Tzu's positive comments in the *Lieh Tzu* about losing his memory: "Formerly, when I forgot, I was boundless; I did not notice whether heaven and earth existed or not" (Graham, 71). Or if, like the Confucian disciple Yen Hui, one engages in "sitting and forgetting" or any similar meditative practice of depth, one will pass through a gate opening out onto a boundless field where one can go "wandering in any far away, carefree, and as-you-like-it paths" (Watson, 1996, 86).

In accord with his spiritual genius, "Chuang Tzu employs the metaphor of a totally free and purposeless journey, using the word *yu* (to wander, or a wandering) to designate the way in which the enlightened [person] wanders through all of creation, enjoying its delights without ever becoming attached to any one part of it" (Watson, 1996, 6). When seemingly simple concepts like forgetting, non-action, wandering, simplicity, etc. are used by Chuang Tzu they adopt a richness of meaning that within a complex web of metaphors and layers of analogy, introduce the elder to ways of knowing and acting that can open him or her to a life filled with "crazy wisdom."

For such an elder, Mair's paraphrase of Chuang Tzu's ideas carries a lot of weight—though with a lightsome, spiritual promise:

> The human form has ten thousand changes that never come to an end. Your joys, then, must be uncountable. Therefore the sage wanders in the realm where things cannot get away from him and all are preserved [which is to] wander beyond the realm of mundane attachment to things or ideas [to] wander free and easy in the service of [non-action]. (Mair, "Wandering," 113)

Freedom is the air the human spirit breathes; imagination and play are wings with which the spirit soars into that air. As Victor Mair notes, "freedom is precious" for Chuang Tzu and is the "keynote" of his entire work. But "how does one become free?" Mair answers: "He does so by unfettering himself from the world and all of its constrictions, conventions, conceptions and material constituents." This sounds like pretty serious and grim work, but Mair insists that for Chuang Tzu, "[t]he only way to accomplish this is by adopting a playful mode of movement." That is, one "learns to 'wander,' as Chuang Tzu states repeatedly" (*"Wandering,"* 107).

III

Free and Easy Wandering

The opening chapter of the *Zhuangzi* is titled *xiaoyaoyou* which Mair translates as "Carefree Wandering" (Mair,3). It begins with a delightful story of the great mythic fish K'un who in the darkness of the Northern

Ocean transforms into "the great P'eng bird" who, in an act of wandering that witnesses to its great freedom, flies vast distances at great heights, even as far as the Southern Ocean or "Lake of Heaven." (Mair, 3).

The final tale of the *Zhuangzi's* first chapter links the theme of "wandering" with that of being "useless." The tale begins with Hui Tzu (Master Hui), the sophist and frequent debater with Chuang Tzu, trying again to negate the usefulness, if not the intelligibility, of Chuang Tzu's teachings. "I have a great tree, the people call it tree-of-heaven," Master Hui declares (Graham, 47). The problem, Hui Tzu laments, is that its trunk is so "knobbly and bumpy," its branches so "curly and crooked," that carpenters won't give it a second look. As a result, everyone considers it useless. Then, referring to Chuang Tzu's philosophy, he says, "Now this talk of yours is big but useless, dismissed by everyone alike" (Graham, 47).

Chuang Tzu immediately responds by drawing Hui Tzu's attention to the small wildcat or weasel that everyone admires because of its great speed, agility and hunting skills. It is able to crouch low and nimbly jump here and there to get to its prey. However, the very qualities that seem so useful and are admired by everyone, prove self-defeating when he "drops plumb into the snare and dies in the net" (Ibid.). Trappers, in other words, find a way to capture the weasel by exploiting (using) its useful but predictable habits. Similarly, there is the yak "which is big as a cloud hanging from the sky," who is admired for its great size but who is useless when it comes to catching rats or mice. Chuang Tzu concludes:

> Now if you have a great tree and think it's a pity it's so useless, why not plant it in the realm of Nothing whatever, in the wilds which spread out into nowhere, and go roaming away [wandering] to do nothing at its side, ramble around [wander] and fall asleep in its shade?

Spared by the axe
No thing will harm it.
If you're no use at all,
Who'll come to bother you? (Graham, 47)

On one level, Chuang Tzu is saying that the uselessness that Hui Tzu considers a negative characteristic has allowed the tree to grow to the point that it can provide space and shade within which a person can "wander" and "play" and even take a nap. The problem with Hui Tzu, Chuang Tzu suggests, is his unimaginative mind. It is locked into the belief that something can be valuable and worthwhile only to the degree that it is deemed "useful" to humans. Such a narrow perspective on and perception of other beings (and nature as a whole), closes off Hui Tzu and others to the experience of qualities that are intrinsic and of spiritual value.

Of course, to one whose mind is fenced in by the parameters of the conventional, the *Chuang Tzu's* teachings will sound crazy, useless and possibly even dangerous. But one who has a free and open mind will excitedly "wander" among Chuang Tzu's metaphors, jokes, exaggerated characters, tall tales, flowering phrases and paradoxical playfulness. In the process one's mind/heart will become further transformed into the equivalent of the great P'eng bird as it takes flight, soaring above the acceptable range of conventional thought. And, as in the P'eng story, there will emerge from the instrumental mentality and parochial spirit of Adulthood, the higher, "useless" mind and spirit of Elderhood which will playfully ramble and wander in the realm of Nothing Whatsoever. A transformation in consciousness will have occurred, one made possible by "forgetting" the many "useful" lures or promises meant to lead Elders into a caged existence advertised as "mature living."

IV

From Brains-of-Brambles to Imaginative Minds

Not internalizing but "forgetting" Adultworld's definitions of and criteria for usefulness, elders can open themselves to dillydallying, wandering, rambling about, and thereby refreshing their hearts and minds by the liberating energies of new growth. Master Hui's inability to open his mind-heart and experience alternatives associated with wandering, freedom, and play is borne out in another anecdote in Chapter One. Here Master Hui informs Master Chuang that "The King of Wei presented me with the seeds of a large gourd" (Mair, 7-8). However, it grew so big that he could make no use of it and so he smashed it into bits and pieces! Chuang Tzu is appalled at the utter lack of imagination and creative thinking evinced here. "Sir," Master Chuang forcefully responds, "it's you who were obtuse about utilizing its bigness," displaying no imagination. Chuang Tzu turns to Hui and pointedly asks him why he didn't think of tying the gourd onto his waist "as a big buoy so that you could go floating on the lakes and rivers instead of worrying that it couldn't hold anything because of its shallow curvature? This shows, sir, that you still have brambles for brains!'" (Mair, 8).

In both stories, Master Hui is chided for his mind's imprisonment within conventional and utilitarian ways of judging the possible use and meaning of things—and of life. His instrumental reason blocked imagination, creativity, and the possibility of real freedom (and fun). This is reflected in his inability to recognize intrinsic value in wandering along the rivers and lakes in a carefree, playful mode. Hui Tzu is offered a hint--which one suspects he does not catch--at the connection between uselessness and the spiritual state designated by terms like "wandering" or "floating." This phase of the spiritual life contains qualities analogous to floating on rivers and lakes. In fact, it resembles the meandering of rivers themselves-- swirling around and over obstacles, avoiding conflict and confrontation.

Rur-Bin-Yang recognizes the importance of *wandering* to capturing the overall mystical journey and dynamic presented by Chuang Tzu / Zhuangzi:

> After one merges the body with the mind, the mind with the vital energy, and the vital energy with the spirit, one's human consciousness and bodily energy will mix and flow together with the vital energy of the cosmos; the mind at such a time we may call the "wandering" (*you*) mind. The term *wandering* is very unique to Zhuangzi's thought. Sometimes we see him using it to describe certain True Men roaming through the lands in all directions . . . this concept, transmitted down from primitive religion, certainly has its reality within the cultural system, and Zhuangzi often makes use of this type of imagery. (Rur-Bin-Yang, in Cook, 112)

Zhuangzi also uses "wandering" to indicate the spiritual state of those who "have joined with the Creator as men to wander in the unitary energy (*yiqi*) of Heaven and Earth" (Ibid.). Or, in terms of absolute uselessness, Zhuangzi suggests in Chapter 20 how different it would be if "you were to climb up on the *Dao* and its Virtue and go drifting and wandering, neither praised or damned, now a dragon, now a snake, shifting with the times, never willing to hold to one course only . . . drifting and wandering with the ancestor of the ten thousand things, treating things as things but not letting them treat you as a thing—then how could you get in trouble?" (tr. Rur-Bin-Yang, in Cook, 112-113). Shifting metaphors, Zhuangzi suggests in Chapter 11 that one should "enter the gate of the inexhaustible and wander in the limitless fields" (tr. Rur-Bin-Yang in Cook, 112).

For Chuang Tzu, when the duality of self and other vanishes as a person merges with the Way and thereby "wanders" in a state above knowledge as we usually conceive of it, this transformed person, upon his or her "return" enters into a transformed world. Roth renders Graham's translation of a section in Chapter Two, "All things whether developing or dissolving revert to being pervaded and unified. Only those who penetrate this know how to pervade and unify things" (Roth, 43). As Roth footnotes:

> [T]he Way pervades everything and in pervading them unifies them. They are unified to the extent that each and every thing contains the Way within it; and they are unified in that, from the perspective of the Way within, each thing is seen to be equal. Because they attain this Way, sages can have the same perspective. (Roth, 43 f.n.61)

Sages, through a discipline of "forgetting," eventually merge with the Way and *wander* as more spontaneous, free, creative people. They have put aside a way of seeing and acting based on a set of conventional concepts, principles and behavioral norms and "flow" freely through and around various situations and circumstances. Roth calls it a more "Way-centered mode of being" and contrasts it with "the ego-centered mode of being in which most of us are enmeshed" (Roth, 44). Anyone familiar with traditions where the spiritual life consists in developing an "inner" contemplative life and integrating it with an "outer" active life will recognize the basic dynamic at play. It can become the way of an Elder who moves into a state of "wandering," abandoning their "ego-centered" mode of being while expanding and opening their selves to the Way which moves through the process of Life, dwells within each being while aiding its harmonious interaction with other beings.

Eugene Bianchi identifies the unique creativity of Elders with the cultivation of their inner resources.

> Creative elders are able to move beyond negative cultural stereotypes of being old by cultivating their inner resources . . . The aesthetic and imaginative dimensions of all the arts are akin to the spiritual because they express the deeper longing of the soul for beauty and meaning . . . Another aspect of cultivating inner resources among creative elders is their ability to cultivate serene self-esteem [and move] from a fear-driven to a love-motivated life. (*The Way*, April 1996, 95)

WORKS CITED

Bianchi, Eugene. *The Way.* April, 1996.

Graham, A.C. *Chuang Tzu: The Inner Chapters.* Second Edition Indianapolis, IN: Hackett Publishing Company, 2001

Mair, Victor H. *Wandering on the Way: Early Taoist Tales and Parables of Chuang Tzu.* New York: Bantam Books, 1994.

Mair, Victor. "Wandering" In Victor H. Mair, (Ed) *Experimental Essays on Chuang Tzu.* Honolulu: University of Hawaii Press, 1983.

Merton, Thomas. *No Man is an Island.* New York: Harvest/HBJ, 1983.

Roth, Harold D. *Original Tao: Inward Training (Nei-yeh) and the Foundations of Taoist Mysticism.* New York: Columbia University Press

Watson, Burton. tr. *Chuang Tzu: Basic Writings.* New York: Columbia University Press, 1996.

Watson, Burton, tr. *The Complete Works of Chuang Tzu*. New York: Columbia University Press, 1968.

Yang, Rur-Bin-, "'From Merging the Body with the Mind' to 'Wandering in Unitary *Qi*': A discussion of Zhuangzi's Realm of the True Man and Its Corporeal Basis" In Scot Cook, editor. *Hiding the World in the World: Uneven Discourses on the Zhunagzi*" (SUNY Series in Chinese Philosophy and Culture) Albany: SUNY Press, 2003, pp. 89-127.

CHAPTER FIVE

The usefulness of the useless

"You have heard of the usefulness of the useful.
It is time to hear of the usefulness of the useless."
The Chuang Tzu 4.9 (My Paraphrase)

Chuang Tzu's praise of uselessness strikes modern sensibilities as extremely bizarre, if not downright dangerous. It threatens the engine of the economy, undermines the work ethic, and upsets one of modern society's basic ideological tools. Teenagers are scolded by Adultworld's gatekeepers and told to "make yourself useful--get a job" or "get an education." And indeed, college students are recruited using the latest figures on how "useful" a so-called "higher" education will prove. One might ask: "Useful to whom?" or "Useful for what?" or "Useful at what personal price?" On the other side of Adulthood, retirees echo this refrain, "My biggest fear is being useless," or, "I don't want to end up a useless old man."

A variation on this theme among retirees is the need to justify their existence by "keeping busy" and, when asked, proclaim that they have never been "*sooo*" busy. An elder's obsession with usefulness and busy-ness reflects the ongoing influence that a "produce-and-consume" economy continues to have on their sense of identity and worth. However, there can be another "way," one that leads to the free spirit of the sagely elder.

I

Trees: Useful and "Useless"

In Chapter Four of the *Chuang Tzu*, Tzu-ch'i of Nan-po was out for a hike in the hills when he suddenly came upon an awesome tree. It was so big that a thousand chariots with four-horse teams could have sheltered in its shade. Being a practical man, he immediately calculated the amount of timber it would yield. However, upon closer examination, he realized that the smaller branches were all twisted and hence worthless for beams, the huge trunk was all gnarled and therefore useless for planks for coffins or similarly shaped products. If you licked its leaves, your mouth developed ulcers; if you took a strong whiff of its foliage, you'd fall into a drunken stupor that lasted for days. "It turns out to be a completely unusable tree," said Tzu-Ch'i, "and so it has been able to grow this big. Aha!— it is this unusableness that the Holy Man makes use of!" (Watson, 61). Or, as Graham translates: "That is why the most daemonic [spiritual] of men are made of such poor stuff!" (Graham, 74).

Interestingly, uselessness was crucial to the tree's awe-inspiring growth. It could grow to its full height because carpenters, tradesmen, and land grabbers could find no useful purpose for it. The tree's seemingly negative qualities saved it from being cut down and, as a result, its potential for growth could be fully realized. Since no one could figure out what to DO with it, it could BE itself. The wise elder, like the tree, is the one who is developing his or her innate abilities or heavenly capacities (*te/de*) to their fullest. The enlightened elder, like the ancient sage, is able to elude the clutches of those social and cultural leaders who want to insist that his or her value still lies in being a socially or economically useful tool, even if "retired."

Following Tzu-Ch'i's comments, the *Chuang Tzu* turns to the various fates of "useful" trees. A small one will be chopped down to make a tether post for a monkey; a medium sized one will be axed to make a ridge-pole for a roof; a large one will be used to make a coffin side-plank. Because of these and many similar "uses," these trees will not realize their innate growth potential which means they will not last out their years "but die in mid-journey under the axe. That is the trouble with being stuff which is good for something" (Graham, 74).

Yet, of course, today's children are warned by their parents, "Don't be a good-for-nothing." The assumption is that they can be a good-for-something by giving themselves over to be "made" into a particular kind of "thing" that can function as part of a particular social machine. It is irrelevant that in becoming a good-for something (an extrinsic instrumental good) you may ignore and/or leave undeveloped important qualities of your own good, i.e. your intrinsic good (*te*). Of course the more utilitarian and materialistic modern belief is that if you look inside yourself in the twin hope of discovering your own spiritually vital powers and developing them to become your own unique **someone** (rather than a some-thing), you will find **nothing**. And out of nothing can only come what is "good for nothing." No suggestion that you might have found something unique and powerful and through it developed into an intrinsically valuable someone.

What the "useful" trees have in common is that their own good (*te*) is not allowed to grow to its fullest extent and, at least for these trees, being useful cuts the lifespan within which this growth could continue. In Taoist terms, this good *(te)* is rooted in and grows through cooperation with the inner potentials and powers of the way of Heaven/Nature. It is no coincidence that for most modern humans, other-than-human beings have no intrinsic value but only instrumental, utilitarian value that centers on their "usefulness": profit, gamesmanship, scientific information, food, etc.

Returning to Chuang Tzu, we might ask him: "If one is to avoid being useful and 'good for something' should one then desire to be useless and 'good for nothing?'" "Not exactly" he might reply.

II

Positive Uselessness

Following its lament for the fate of useful trees, the *Chuang Tzu* shifts its attention to a river where religious officials are sacrificing animals (and humans?) to the river spirit. Most qualify for the dubious value as "stuff which is good for something" (Graham, 74). However, in these sacrifices,

. . . it is forbidden to cast into the waters an ox with a white forehead, a pig with a turned-up snout or a man with piles. These are all known to be exempt by shamans and priests, being things they deem bearers of ill-luck. They are the very things which the daemonic man [spiritual person] will deem supremely lucky. (Graham, 74)

Chuang Tzu is also alluding to the sacrifices that political and economic systems make to the gods of power and wealth. Certain human traits and skills and talents are valuable and useful, while others are valueless and dismissed. The abnormal physical characteristics of the ox, pig, and human in the narrative "saves" them from the honor of being "sacrificed" to a higher power. The spiritual person that Chuang Tzu praises does not refer to a "man of spirits" like the shaman who recruits victims useful for sacrifice and hence for material blessings for sponsors from the river god. Rather, he is a sage who realizes that those unique or "abnormal" traits that made certain beings useless as sacrificial victims for the increased material welfare and religious orthodoxy of the sponsors, protected and allowed for the further realization of their individual authenticity and integrity (*te*). Chuang Tzu challenges society's major beliefs and practices in order to free the self from its dependence on cultural definitions of identity and worth tied to wider economic and social institutions. Society is too eager to link "abnormal" traits to judgments about a person's usefulness.

Many elders judge themselves too harshly, criticizing those personal traits that had allegedly kept them from the lucrative career or attractive mate. They say, "I was useless" or "My life was a waste." But perhaps what appeared to be the effect of personal flaws or psychological oddities that sent them on a different path may have been blessings in disguise that invited them to listen to their own deeper voices. The ensuing path was more truly their own. Their so-called "oddities" actually guarded and protected their emerging spiritual capacities. In the story, the spiritual person does not dabble in lower forms of magic or trance-states like the shamans and priests. If his "odd" traits are judged as "flaws" to his character and thus make him "useless" in terms of what river gods and superstitious patrons desire, the sage or spiritual person sees them within a deeper context as bearers of good luck to their possessors. Chuang Tzu wants us to look more carefully at the advantages that ill-omened marks have for certain animals. He then draws an analogy to what happens to humans with unconventional traits whose uselessness proves quite useful.

III

Being "Different And Useless" Can Turn Out To Be Useful

The following story, found in Chapter Four, is about an ill-omened man and the result of his being deemed useless. We then return to the trees for a higher climb into the meaning of uselessness.

Chuang Tzu describes a physically misshapen man named Cripple Shu:

> ...His chin is buried down in his navel, his shoulders are higher than his crown, the knobbly bone at the base of his neck points at the sky, the five pipes to the spine are right up on top, his two thigh bones make another pair of ribs. (Graham, 74)

Our attention, like that of his contemporaries, is immediately drawn to the extremely unusual composition of Shu's body. Our pity goes out to him. He is unable to do many of the things that other young men can do. He is "different", so different that one is impressed by the fact that he can make a living at all. One day, military recruiters visit the village looking for "a few good men," as we would say, who have the "right stuff." That is, they are strong, coordinated, trainable, a bit reckless and full of youthful dreams of heroism. Such men will look impressive on the parade ground dressed in identical uniforms, standing erect, swinging weapons and stomping their boots in unison. But then there is Shu, shuffling around, "flipping back his sleeves" to bare his arms (Graham, 74). He is definitely not military material. He would be an embarrassment to the rank-and-file: out of step, swinging arms wildly, grunting loudly and dragging his feet clumsily. In battle he would need to be protected by his own men lest he be slain by the first enemy soldier to face him. As a consequence, he will just have to miss the adulation of the old men, the swooning of the young women, and the honor of dying for his country (or King). Of course, his uselessness to the military proves extremely useful to him.

A similar situation unfolds when the public works administrators come to recruit laborers for highway construction and other state projects. Shu is eliminated because of a litany of ailments. While work gang positions were not as esteemed as those of soldiers, the "volunteers" might console themselves in the knowledge that in serving the common good they had found usefulness and purpose. Afterall, roads brought "progress," allowing merchants to move goods and the state to move troops more swiftly. Throughout history, those with economic or political power made fortunes and reputations with such projects. Of course, a Taoist might point out that this kind of work also takes its toll on men's health, repaying them for their usefulness with a shorter, more stressful and difficult life.

Having been certified as officially useless by both the military and civilian branches of government, Shu became an object of public largesse. Being "cursed" with not just one but multiple "handicaps," he received a proportionately higher amount of public assistance. Furthermore, although Chuang Tzu doesn't mention this, one can only assume that when so many young men did not return from the frontier, as was often the case, a number of attractive single women took a second look at Shu who now was well provided-for and could therefore provide well for a wife--or two.

What is the point of this simple tale? Obviously it warns against making hasty judgments. This story also resembles the host of stories featuring bizarre, strange or monstrous individuals that Chuang Tzu uses to make other points about the superficiality of common tastes and opinions. And although Shu could support himself and a few others by menial labor, his unusual physical traits made him of no "use" to recruiters needing normal capabilities. Nevertheless, Shu's "doing" was an expression of his being and as such enabled him to live out the days allotted to him by Heaven/Nature (*T'ien*). This is also a metaphor for the spiritual life of sagely elders and others whose values, views and even looks are considered "abnormal." They do not conform to nor easily fit into a society whose values center on conformity to conventional tastes and to profit, power, and the reduction of beings of innate goodness to socially useful tools.

What if Shu had allowed himself to become depressed over his crippled body and his being judged "useless"? Shu, however, never complains but realizes that his "handicaps" have saved him. Of course, if one looks more closely, Shu's uselessness and hence resultant good fortune were *relative* to the needs of the social institutions. Is there perhaps something deeper in Chuang Tzu's concept of uselessness? There is another story in Chapter Four that might give us a clue.

IV

A Sacred Uselessnes

Once upon a time, Carpenter Shih and his apprentice were on a journey to Ch'i. when they passed an enormous shrine tree. The oak was so wide that thousands of oxen could stand beneath it. And high? Its lowest branches were eighty feet above the ground, while its peak was as tall as that of a hill. Scores of people just stood around and gazed at it. Master Shih, however, simply walked on by at a brisk pace. In awe, Shih's apprentice stopped to survey the tree. Hurrying to catch up with his master, the apprentice expressed his dismay. Why would a carpenter pass by a tree that could obviously offer so much? His master angrily barked out that it was "good for nothing wood... wretched timber, useless for anything; that's why it's been able to grow so old" (Graham, 73).

That night, the tree appeared to Shih in a dream and criticized him for unfairly comparing it to other trees. The shrine tree pointed out that, ironically, the fruit trees that Shih thought so highly of, lived for only half of their allotted time. Pickers abused them, breaking off their branches and tearing off their limbs as they grabbed for their fruit. But it wasn't totally the pickers' fault. The fruit trees had brought this upon themselves. By their own "abilities" they "make life miserable for themselves" and die prematurely. By advertising their beautiful blossoms and delicious-looking fruit they "let themselves be made victims of worldly vulgarity" (Graham, 73).

The elder shrine tree then opens Shih's eyes to the heart of the issue. Good fortune had not befallen it simply due to good luck. The tree had intentionally tried for most of its life "to become of no possible use to anyone." Now, nearing death, it had achieved *absolute uselessness* that ironically proved "supremely useful." If it had tried to be useful like the other trees, would it "have had the opportunity to grow so big?" (Graham, 73). The tree then criticizes the audacity of the carpenter, claiming that he, a good for nothing human, had no right to call it a "good for nothing," defective, and useless tree. The carpenter is a flawed mortal and is himself close to death. Something clicked in the mind of the carpenter; something that shattered all of his comfortable, conventional illusions. The carpenter began to see the significance of the oak tree's uselessness to his own life.

His apprentice, however, criticized the tree's remarks, pointing out the contradiction between its claim to having pursued uselessness and its *de facto* usefulness as a shrine tree. The carpenter revealed the depth of his own insight. In a loud, emphatic voice he told his apprentice to shut up and listen:

"The oak is merely assuming the guise of a shrine to ward off the curses of those who do not understand it" (Mair, 38). Being a shrine tree frees it from judgments of useful or useless. And he warns that no one can understand it using conventional thought or ethic.

The tree had told the carpenter that when it was still a young tree it had made a deliberate effort to be useless. By adopting undesirable features, the oak had managed to escape the crafty, scheming eyes of woodsmen and craftsmen like Shih. Uselessness was a means to an end, and the ultimate end, the oak had thought at the time, was survival. Although its uselessness was tenuous, this development guarded the tree's life. Thus the tree was able to spread its limbs, deepen its roots, and grow into its full potential. "Finally, on the verge of death," the oak has realized what uselessness really means and that that realization is of great use to it (Mair, 38).

Why only now, as an elder tree, had it realized this deeper truth? Perhaps the oak realized that relative uselessness still remained too useful. Adopting the guise of uselessness, it had attained a certain freedom-from the shaping and mis-shaping forces of society. But more importantly, he developed a freedom-for growth and spiritual development and the latter had led to a breakthrough. In becoming an end in itself, uselessness took on a whole new dimension. As Shih had said, "what the oak is preserving is different from the masses of other trees" (Ibid.).

We should note that in becoming a shrine tree, the oak had become an embodiment of the sacred. The oak had discovered a realm of freedom and a spiritual or cosmic identity that transcended both the apprentice's judgment of "useful" and carpenter Shih's of "useless" while protecting it against those bitter individuals who might, upon discovering that it was useless, curse it and cut it down out of spite. Transcendental or absolute uselessness and the accompanying level of self-realization and positive freedom no longer depended on its having or not having particular physical features.

Being sacred was what made the oak and its uselessness different. What it was "preserving," while keeping it hidden, escaped conventional thinking. Perhaps the people who gazed in awe and wonder at the elder shrine tree intuited something of that. Was not the sacred precinct, which the altar and the tree marked off, a holy space free from mundane values and where judgments of useful and useless were not permitted (or did not even arise?).

Perhaps elders are also called upon to be liminal beings. In traditional cultures, a liminal being was one who stood between and mediated the conventional social world and the sacred cosmos that supported and vivified it. Just as an infant comes into this human world trailing clouds of glory, still cloaked with cosmic mystery, so an elder can step to the edge of this world in order to apprehend, experience and communicate back something of a deeper reality. Did the tree not suggest that Carpenter Shih take the fact that he was a mortal on the verge of death seriously and learn from the tree?

What the infant and the elder witness to is that wild, spontaneous cosmos filled with intrinsic value. It transcends definitions of useful and useless as do those who participate in its higher levels of Being. Apprehending it requires "only" the pure and innocent heart of a child and the deep and wise mind of an elder.

The many aphorisms and dire warnings that some parents use to bring their children back "in-line," often serve to prepare them for the modern social version of carpenters and wood carvers. While children may have a more difficult time resisting or even imagining an alternative to this fate, elders should know better. Yet, both a child and an elder carry within themselves echoes of Adultworld's voices warning of the dire consequences of uselessness. In this they share the same anxiety. Children carry it as a reminder of what they yet lack; older adults and elders carry it as a reminder of what they should not give up. And there are the voices of anti-retirement gurus who preach "Be useful 'til you drop." In other words, keep your old job or at least get a new one that resembles it. Some psychological carpenters insist that your "real age" is ten years younger than your chronological age, implying that you are really still an adult, so "why retire?" This plan might be called, "No adult left behind."

What can elders (and some children) learn from the stories of crippled Shu and the twisted oak? One lesson might be to adopt the "relative uselessness" of the younger oak and Shu. This could buy time and create the conditions necessary for a more genuine and personally fuller growth--and lead to the realization of an *absolute* uselessness that the older tree confesses is paradoxically also truly useful. Chuang Tzu reveals more of what this might mean in a story that includes himself.

V

Drifting and Wandering Beyond Useful and Useless

At the beginning of Chapter Twenty, we find Chuang Tzu and his disciples hiking through the mountains where they come upon a lumberman standing by a huge fully-grown tree. He had decided not to cut it down because he judged that there was nothing it could be used for. Chuang Tzu reminded his disciples that it was precisely because of its uselessness that the tree was "able to live out all of the years allotted to it by heaven..." (Mair,185).

Coming down from the mountain, Master Chuang decided to lodge with his disciples "in the home of an old friend" who served as their host. The host ordered a boy to kill and then cook a goose. But there were two geese: one that cackled and one that did not. Needing to make a decision, the host decided to sacrifice the one who couldn't cackle. Needless to say, Chuang Tzu's disciples were confused as to why uselessness had worked to protect the tree but not to save the goose. They asked their Master whether he would rather be in the condition of the useful goose (and live) or the useless goose and have his life shortened. He laughed, suggesting that one alternative might be to pick a position "somewhere between worthlessness and worthiness" (Mair,187). (Some readers might suggest that this strategy is more realistic for elders.) Yet, Chuang Tzu had to admit that that position was itself not easy to maintain and would not prevent trouble from arising. What could? He takes them higher.

> One who takes his seat on the Tao and its attributes [Virtue], and there finds his ease and enjoyment, is not exposed to such a contingency. He is above the reach of both praise and detraction. Now he mounts aloft like a dragon; now he keeps beneath like a snake. He is transformed with the changing character of the time and is not willing to addict himself to any one thing. Now in a high position and now in a low, he is in harmony with all his surroundings; he enjoys himself at ease with the Author [Ancestor] of all things; he treats things as things and is not a thing to them: where is his liability to be in trouble? (Waltham/Legge, 225)

One can *wander* as one pleases, now being useless, then being useful, but bound by neither. One can be useful without being used (like a thing) and one can be useless without needing to compare oneself with others. True or absolute uselessness is a radical freedom that transcends social uselessness and is experienced as a state of "wandering," another elder phenomenon.

Chuang Tzu's phrase, "never willing to hold to one course only," implies that one can drift and wander, "now up, now down, taking harmony for your measure" in accord with the Ancestor of everything (*Tao*). In one situation you are a dragon, in another, a snake, "shifting with the times." Without set form you are not a "thing" or "object" that can be neatly categorized but a free, formless, "subject" with an adaptable spirit and consciousness. One can surmise that Chuang Tzu is also advocating flexibility of mind, rather than the taking of a set position on "this" or "that." One is not bound by either and is free to take either or both. *It is what is harmonious--not what is absolutely true or false; what is more contextual, not a preconceived convention imposed on every situation.*

I recently overheard an adult brother complain to his sister: "I don't know what to make of Mom anymore." Sounds like Hui Tzu complaining about his gourd! The words "to make" and "anymore" are telling. What is implied is: "Up until now both society and her children have been able to 'make' this person into something 'useful': mother, wife, cook, chauffeur, teacher, church volunteer, etc." Now she seems to be doing and saying things that don't fit the once "useful" roles assigned to her. She won't allow them to define her "anymore." Carpenter Shih's words about the sacred tree come to mind: "There's nothing you can make from it. That's why it could grow to be so old" (Mair, 37). For a human it could mean "using" your time to explore your overlooked or heretofore socially restricted potentials.

In the midst of her children's conversation, I felt like saying: "Perhaps, just perhaps, she is trying to imaginatively and creatively explore some of those inner resources that she was forced to ignore so she could respond to other peoples' demands. Perhaps she wants to draw upon and express her own unique inner powers.

Rather than complain, her children should rejoice that their mother's inner spirit has not been destroyed by the cult of usefulness but remains alive and capable of development. Let her grow into Hui Tzu's useless tree! Quit molding, shaping and carving her up! To say that, "Sometimes we don't know WHO she is," may be to acknowledge the emergence of a dimension of her that has been hiding behind or beneath the many selves defined by her various roles. Let the children lighten up; let her find her inner stillness and ripen so she may come forth to "comfort" us of this era or age.

In Chapter Thirteen, Chuang Tzu states that a sage "waits on all things" until the time is ripe to express him or herself and to act:

> The still mind of the sage is the mirror of heaven and earth, the glass of all things. Vacancy, stillness, placidity, tastelessness, quietude, silence, and nonaction: this is the level of heaven and earth and the perfection of the Tao and its characteristics . . .
>
> Vacancy, stillness, placidity, tastelessness, quietude, silence, and doing-nothing are the root of all things . . . With this root, retiring from public life and enjoying themselves at leisure, we find the scholars who dwell by the rivers and seas, among the hills and forests, all submissive to it; with this root coming forward to active life and comforting their age, their merit is great, and their fame is distinguished; all the world becomes united in one. (Waltham/Legge, 157-158)

VI

Some Concluding Thoughts

As adults we were taught the usefulness of the useful, but now it is time to learn the usefulness of the useless! Not only to learn it, but to live it, and to teach it out of compassion to children and to adults with flexible, adventurous minds.

First, you must look inside and rediscover your useless dimension (never fully lost), your inner Voice which wants to express itself with special power and beauty at this stage in life. Listen deeply, walk slowly, mellow gracefully, return to and deepen your *being*. Then, as it ripens, move out to a doing. This time it is a doing that flows from and remains rooted in your being. One might call it an Action rooted in and expressive of Contemplation. Useful do-ing, including mental activity, no longer takes you outside of your be-ing. You are not an "object." So you are sensitive to others and can enter into non-coercive relationships. You are unlike the children who I heard complaining about not knowing what "to make" of Mom. You see more deeply into what others are and are becoming. Perhaps also into what or who are stunting her growth.

Refuse to make comparisons between who you are now and who you were at forty or fifty. Rather than allow others or your earlier self to set the ground rules for you, turn the table on them. As an elder, be a model of the qualities **they** should be developing already. Invite them to grow intellectually, imaginatively and spiritually (in the subtle energy of their wholeness). Urge them on so that they will begin to transcend Adulthood with its wearisome incantations to work long hours and buy happiness. Help them examine their own obsessions with being socially or economically "useful." Elders are being called upon to serve as reminders that humankind's potentials lie beyond pushing papers, fighting wars and consuming products.

Being still is useless. Be still. Dancing is useless. Dance! Painting is useless. Paint! Playing is useless, making love is useless, meditating is useless; praying is useless; celebrating liturgies is useless; and, in fact, life itself is useless--which is its ultimate saving power. The problem with many adult religious people is not that they engage in rituals or prayer but that they do these things because they consider them profitable for themselves. Perhaps celebrations, prayers, meditations are what humans do as part of the cosmos, the equivalent of riding the winds for eagles and leaping out of the water for dolphins, or exploding for super-nova.

WORKS CITED

Graham, A.C. *Chuang Tzu: The Inner Chapters.* Second Edition Indianapolis, IN: Hackett Publishing Company, 2001

Mair, Victor H. tr. *Wandering on the Way: Early Taoist Tales and Parables of Chuang Tzu.* New York: Bantam Books, 1994.

Waltham, Clae, Editor and James Legge, translator. *Chuang Tzu: Genius of the Absurd.* New York: Ace Books, 1971.

Watson, Burton, tr. *Chuang Tzu: Basic Writings.* New York: Columbia Univ. Press, 1964.

CHAPTER SIX

Elderway, Waterway

"Fish forget themselves in water, humans forget themselves in Dao."

Water imagery abounds and flows everywhere in Taoism/Daoism. An elder should reflect on, take to heart, and venture to practice the water wisdom found in the *Chuang Tzu*. But earlier, Lao Tzu in the classic *Tao te Ching/daodejing*, laid out many beautiful and intriguing suggestions about how the qualities and actions of water can, through metaphorical application to humans, be a source of crazy wisdom.

> There is nothing softer or weaker than water
> And yet there is nothing better for attacking hard and
> strong things
> For this reason there is no substitute for it.

All the world knows that the weak overcomes the strong
   and the soft overcomes the hard.
But none can practice it . . .

Therefore, straight words seem to be crooked
                                    Tao te Ching Ch.78 (Chan)

Note: let the crazy wisdom of elders with its seemingly crooked words be epitomized through actions and ideas that are not wedded to images of being tough, rough, hard, and unyielding but instead secretly married to the soft, life- giving and mysteriously effective ways of water. At the center of many of Chuang Tzu's stories is an elder who lives on or near the water including one engaged in diving with a waterfall from very high cliffs. Some others ferry boats, fish without hooks, etc. Still learning water's ways, they learn deeper truths about living life so as to be renewed by Tao's energy. This is contrasted with a Confucian vision and way of life that relies on a well-ordered, more conformist society that rewards its members who have practiced, incorporated into their behavior and now display through their lives the principal Confucian virtues.

Through their experience with and in water, many of Chuang Tzu's sages learn "new ways" of anticipating and responding to life's changes in-synch with and under the guiding movement of Tao. The adult denizens of conventionality often find themselves perplexed and speechless or at least defensively dogmatic when confronted with these incarnations of waterways.

I

A Spirit-like Ferryman

Chapter Nineteen opens with a disciple of Confucius named Yen Yuan telling his Master that he had been awe-struck at the sight of a spirit-like ferryman who handled his boat "with supernatural skill" (Watson, 121). He then asked the ferryman if his skill could be learned. As a fledgling Confucianist Yen undoubtedly assumed that if that were the case, then the "method" could be taught to anyone and hence anyone could learn to pilot a boat with seemingly "supernatural skill." The ferryman confessed that a good swimmer could probably learn rather quickly how to handle a boat; a person who could swim smoothly under water, even if he had never seen a boat, could handle it immediately. When Yen asked the ferryman why this was so, he received no reply. Yen asked Confucius if he knew what the ferryman had meant (Mair, 323).

The Taoist-sounding Confucius said that a good swimmer can handle a boat with ease because, through his practice, he "has forgotten the water." (The practice of "forgetting" shows up again, not as "sitting and forgetting", but "swimming and forgetting"). Confucius reasons that someone who can swim under water with great ease is so familiar with the "watery depths" that it is like dry land to him and so he would be no more afraid of the boat capsizing than of a cart turning over. Even if the "10,000 things" were "capsizing" and turning upside down, he would not be affected on the inside—"so where could he go and not be at ease?" His heart would not be anxious or fearful and he would remain relaxed no matter what happened around him (Watson, 121-122).

Elaborating on this inner calm and centeredness, Confucius points out that if you are an archer who simply competes for tiles, "you shoot with skill." But if you are shooting for "fancy belt buckles, you worry about your aim." And if you compete for gold, "you're a nervous wreck." While your skill is the same in all three instances, your inner mental and emotional condition changes as the value of the external prize changes. You "let outside considerations weigh on your mind." Just as the swimmer doesn't allow the capsizing of a boat to disturb his inner composure, so the archer's inner poise and peace would not be swayed by changes in the value of the prize. Confucius ends with a truism: "He who looks too hard at the outside gets clumsy on the inside" (Watson, 122).

II

A Waterfall-Diving, Whirlpool-Swimming Elder

We meet Confucius again in Chapter Nineteen as he encounters another elder associated with water and its ways. (A very similar story appears in Chapter Two of the *Lieh/Liezi*). While out sightseeing, Confucius comes upon a dramatic waterfall that plunges nearly two hundred feet from the top of a cliff into the mists of a dramatically roiling and swirling whirlpool. No turtle, alligator, or even a fish could swim in that torrent, he conjectures. However, as Confucius looks up, an old man dives with the waterfall into the whirlpool and begins swimming right into the misty midst of it. Assuming that the old man is attempting suicide, Confucius orders his disciples to rescue the man. However, as they race along the shore, the man swims another several hundred yards and comes out of the water by himself. In a good mood, he wanders alone beneath the cliffs, happily singing to himself (Watson, 126).

Confucius hurries after him, asking the elder whether he has some particular "method" for floating on and treading in the water. The old man announces that, when he enters the center of the whirlpool, he makes himself a friend of the water and follows *its* way rather than impose himself upon it. He notes that having been born within the surrounding hills he felt secure—that was innate; having grown up in the water he also felt secure—that was his nature. His destiny is to be able to do what he does and how he does it.

So the elder could merge with the water without experiencing fear. Security came from feeling at home among the hills and comfortable in the water. Years of experience sensitized him to changes in the currents. He "forgot" both himself and the water and hence any attitude of fear or enmity that would come between them. If we substitute "life" for "water," we have a model for growing into Elderhood while developing the instincts and abilities that allow us to adjust without fear to life's changing currents. We can feel comfortable with ourselves and with what is our destiny, without the need to gain a sense of self-worth by exaggerating either our positive virtues or the negative qualities of others.

Elsewhere, Chuang Tzu notes that humans are in Tao as fish are in water:

Fishes are born in water
Man is born in Tao . . .
Sinks into the deep shadow
Of non-action
To forget aggression and concern
He lacks nothing
His life is secure. (Merton, 65)

What is the lesson arising from this analogy? "All the fish needs/is to get lost in water./All man needs is to get lost/in Tao" (Ibid.).

This secure ease comes from "forgetting" one's need to compare self with others while at the same time deepening one's security while widening one's identity. Tao becomes one's "second nature." Hence, the True Man can go anywhere, encounter all kinds of changes and transformations, capsizings and near-disasters while remaining relaxed and free within because his life is lived from and at a deeper level.

What kind of spirituality is this? We are given further clues when, at the beginning of section two of Chapter Nineteen, Sir Master Lieh asks Director Yin how it can be that "The perfect [ultimate] man walks under water without encountering any obstruction, treads on fire without being burned, and walks on high above all things without any fear" (Waltham, 213). Yin replies, "It is by his keeping of the pure breath of life [his vital breath]; it is not to be described as an achievement of his skill or daring" (Waltham, 213). Later Yin suggests that a true sage can "unify his nature, nourish his [vital] breath, and unite his Virtue [integrity] and thereby communicate with that which creates all things. A man like this guards what belongs to Heaven and keeps it whole. His spirit has no flaw, so how can things enter in and get at him?" (Watson, 119).

Yin, Director of the Pass, points out that while a drunk can fall from a moving wagon without getting hurt, a sober person who experiences a similar fall could be seriously injured. Both the drunk and the sober person have the same joints and bones, he points out, but the drunk's injuries are "different" because his "spirit is entire." "The thought of death or life, or of any alarm or affright, does not enter his breast. Therefore he encounters danger without shrinking from it." So would a person be towards life who is under the influence of "his Heavenly constitution" (Waltham, 214).

On the one hand, those adults who are the equivalent of the "sober person" take the bumpy wagon ride of life while constantly clinging onto wealth, success or power---afraid to let go. On the other hand, the sagely elder can experience a sense of peace, calm, and security emanating from his or her wholeness of spirit. Or, put another way, to fret and obsess about drowning, falling, or missing the target can create stress, tension and a type of self-consciousness that will bring about the results one has tried so hard to avoid. So it is with life. To forget the target and forget the shooting and forget the shooter is to be present in a totally different "way."

A swimmer forgets the water when it becomes the element within which he moves and breathes and has his being. When he first started swimming, he undoubtedly remembered the water and remembered that he was a human and not a fish. When the water was troubled or the waves were high, he remembered this and fear grew. He mentally separated himself from his immersion in the water. Paradoxically, concern for his own welfare made his welfare more precarious because it blocked him from experiencing the naturalness and fluidity of his usual swimming style. If, however, he forgot himself and relaxed into the water, if he trusted his instincts and was openly sensitive to the water, he understood the power of the water to support him. He lost his fear and spontaneously moved with the water's movements.

The swimmer does not "forget" how to swim or when to respond by striking and when by relaxing. His body and mind are unified as are he and the water. Self-consciousness or obsessions over past mishaps would be disastrous. Likewise, many elders have developed sophisticated patterns of knowing and doing that settled within their constitution over long years of experience with life. What they need to forget are the myriad people and events that had opposed those patterns. Types of meditation, whether while sitting or moving in a special way (*tao*) can aid in a resurrection of a sense of wholeness and fluidity that connects both inner integrity and peace with a sensitivity to changes in the larger whole of which one is a part.

III

Elder Wisdom Walks Out of the Water

In Chapter Thirty-One, Chuang Tzu contrasts the dry-land conventionality of Confucianism with the watery heresy of Taoism. Followers of Confucius are relaxing and reading on top of a riverbank. Their Master is not far away, playing his lute and singing. Unexpectedly, an elder fisherman poles towards them and disembarks from his boat. "His beard and eyebrows were turning white; his hair was all uncombed; his sleeves hung idly down" (Waltham, 351). He climbs up the riverbank and engages the students in a series of questions and comments about their Master. He receives a lengthy litany praising Confucius' personal virtues and his commitment to improving society and government. Surprisingly, the old man expresses concern about Confucius: "By embittering his mind and toiling his body," the elder fisherman warns, "he is imperiling his true nature! Alas! How far removed is he from the proper way of life!' (Waltham, 352).

Shortly thereafter, when told by his followers of their conversation with the fisherman, Confucius declares that the old man must be a sage and rushes to meet him just as he is about to pole his boat away into the marsh. The fisherman turns around. Confucius bows deeply, and with great humility begs to be taught by him, trusting that even at age sixty-nine, he (Confucius) might finally hear the ultimate teaching.

Ironically, the old fisherman proceeds to wax eloquently and at great length on all of the subjects that Confucius had studied and taught for most of his life. Confucius agrees but confesses that he cannot understand why, in his endeavor to teach and to do good to others, he had barely escaped with his life on several occasions. The old man chides Confucius for his overactive, officious and paradoxically self-serving mission. He points out that people tend to resent the many judgments, criticisms and lengthy words of advice being directed at them. What makes it worse is the fact that they come from someone who holds no position of power but has appointed himself the grand educator and chief moral advisor of both ordinary people and the royalty. The watery elder suggests that Confucius really has everything backwards. Because of that, the harder he tries, the worse things get.

He compares Confucius' frantic efforts to those of a person who is so afraid of his shadow and full of antipathy for his footprints that he runs faster and faster in an effort to escape them both. Ultimately the poor soul simply dies from exhaustion. His attempted solutions simply made the problems worse. If he stayed in the shade he could lose his shadow, if he stayed still he could eliminate the need for footprints. But, unfortunately, "His stupidity was excessive!" (Waltham, 355).

Similarly, whenever Confucius finds his life in turmoil and his society in disorder, his reaction is to try harder and harder to control, regulate, and impose constraints on emotions, to rigorously push the practice of virtues and to give altruistic advice to the ruling class. What is the elder fisherman's advice? "Diligently cultivate your person; attentively guard your true nature; let things return to the keeping of others—then there will be nothing in which you will be implicated" (Mair, 321).

Confucius wants to know what his "true nature" is. "One's true nature," declares the fisherman, "is the ultimate expression of pure sincerity. If one is neither pure nor sincere, one cannot move others" (Ibid). Confucius' actions do not spring from or reflect a sincere and selfless (pure) inner state (his true nature) because he did not engage in the inner work necessary to develop it. As a result, he has to feign expressions of sadness or anger or affection. Such superficiality cannot really move or motivate others.

The elder fisherman sees Confucius as one who attempts to teach people how to initiate and properly display externally rehearsed and socially approved behavior. He, on the other hand, maintains that people should be encouraged to develop an inner purity, integrity, and sincerity that can then be subtly released and truly affect others. Rooted in truth and one's true nature, one can flow like water, responding and reacting spontaneously to all the varied relationships and situations in which one finds one self.

The fisherman complains that the emotions and behaviors of most people are overly influenced by other people and by social customs. They don't look deeply enough into themselves and hence miss a deeper, broader and yet more personally supportive energy (like a fisherman's boat buoyed and moved by the water). They don't develop their own true nature that would take its guidance from Heaven *(tian)* or *Dao/Tao*. Consequently, they feel incomplete because their source of self-affirmation is incomplete. The old fisherman expresses pity that Confucius has spent so much of his life dabbling into secondary things and only, as of late, has come to know about The Great Way or Dao (Waltham, 357).

Confucius begs to be allowed to complete his understanding of the Way under the tutelage of the fisherman. The latter, not seeming to want to start a school of the Way and be an official teacher in it, tells Confucius that he must leave but that Confucius must "exert" himself. Having said that, he shoves off and poles his boat through the green reeds. Confucius stands still, oblivious to his students. Once the poling could no longer be heard or ripples seen, he climbed into his carriage. (Mair, 323).

The old man believed strongly that one can live the "heavenly" Way in the human world. But to do that, one must return to the Source within, make one's self sincere, rediscover one's true nature, and then act by non-acting, i.e. spontaneously. This will enable an elder, for example, to adjust whatever he or she is doing so that it responds to this guiding impulse. Confucius rejects his students' complaints that he has humbled himself too much before the fisherman, insisting that he is a true sage, an ultimate man. "Therefore, wherever the Way exists, the sage honors it. Now, we may say that the old fisherman possesses the Way. Dare I not respect him?" (Mair, 323).

We can say that just as when this fisherman's boat heads out into the water, his inner freedom and wisdom expand. Likewise, an elder no longer holds onto the shore of Adultworld or fights the move into the waters of Elderhood. He or she "lets go of" the prejudices, preferences, opinions, gripes, and grudges of life on the shore and the in-land of Adultworld. Rather than impatiently swinging an oar or cursing aloud like a fossilized grouch, the elder is relaxed and moves away. Moving out past the shallows, the elder moves into deeper waters where ancient creatures swim in the mysterious dark depths, not concerned with making a splash.

IV

Eternal Fishing

In Chapter Twenty-One of the *Chuang Tzu/Zhuangzi* we meet King Wen who was "sightseeing" at Tsang when he came across an old fisherman whose line had no hook on it. It was, therefore, "an eternal fishing" (Mair, 205). King Wen was deeply impressed and thought of appointing him to a high office and allowing him to be in charge of the government. At first he was afraid that this would not be acceptable to his seniors. But eventually he found a way to get them to accept this old fisherman. Unbelievably, within three years corruption had ceased and the common good was pursued by all without thought of class or rank. Yet the elder had neither changed the laws nor issued his own edicts (Mair, 205-206).

When King Wen had observed the elder's way *(dao)* of fishing, he was convinced that the elder would excel at ruling. A good fisher is like a good ruler: patient, watchful, and free from compulsion. His heart rests in Dao and his mind is enlightened and broad. He identifies himself with fish and water just as a minister identifies himself with the people and their common good. That is, his actions respond to and subtly play with change, but do not interfere with the harmony of the whole. He avoids passing laws and using other methods that would "hook" the people. Hence they can be themselves, individually and communally. In short, the fisher had ruled through non-ruling.

When individuals adapt to *Dao*, a rich communal life develops spontaneously. Abandoning the power of rank and privilege, they return to simplicity and harmony. They emphasize cooperation rather than hierarchical competition. The old man knew the fish and swam among them in spirit just as he and his people would move together in and with *Dao*.

Some shore walkers make the judgment that these people have gone off "the deep end" and have been swallowed up, probably never to return. Shore walkers should be cautious in their judgments about what might lie in these depths and perhaps seek ways of entering the depths themselves. The life-spirit fills the waters with the renewing wisdom and energy needed for "deep fishing" or "eternal-fishing".

The American Sage Henry David Thoreau, understood "deep fishing" and the deep truths that could be experienced from the ways of water. (I thank Krill Ole Thompson for drawing this quote from *Walden* to my attention in his essay cited below).

> Time is but a stream I go a-fishing in. I drink at it; but while I drink I see the sandy bottom and detect how shallow it is. Its thin current slides away, but eternity remains. I would drink deeper; fish in the sky, whose bottom is pebbly with stars. I cannot count one. I know not the first letter of the alphabet. I have always been regretting that I am not as wise as the day I was born . . . (quoted by Thompson in Ames, 32-33)

WORKS CITED

Mair, Victor H. *Wandering on the Way, Early Taoist Tales and Parables of Chuang Tzu*. New York: Bantam Books, 1994.

Merton, Thomas. *The Way of Chuang Tzu*. New York: New Directions Publishing Corp., 1965.

Thompson, Kirill Ole, "What Is the Reason of Failure or Success? The Fisherman's Song Goes Deep into the River" in Ames, Roger T. *Wandering at Ease in the Zhuangzi*. SUNY Press (1998) pp. 15-34.

Waltham, Clae, Editor and James Legge, translator. *Chuang Tzu: Genius of the Absurd*. New York: Ace Books, 1971.

Watson, Burton. *Chuang Tzu: Basic Writings*. New York: Columbia University Press, 1996.

CHAPTER SEVEN

Ways and the Way

Early Daoists were attentive observers of animals and admired how they embodied and expressed the Way through their spontaneous, natural, and mostly non-reflective behaviors. The result was a display of seemingly effortless, yet concentrated, grace and power. Their performance was a spontaneous work of art that "fit" into a larger whole while contributing a distinctive voice to a rich eco-harmony. While moving with its natural instincts and dispositions, a tiger simultaneously manifests its own innate power (*de*) and contributes to the larger dynamic Way (*Dao*) of Nature or Heaven (*tian*). Daoists were convinced that humans were called upon to find their own kind of "natural," spontaneous life-ways that were an expression and fulfillment of their original nature (*xing*), a participation in the dance of the ten-thousand or myriad things, and an integration into and manifestation of the Great Way (*Dao*). The various abilities and qualities of animals, plants, insects, rivers, streams, etc. have always had something to teach humans. To say that the myriad beings act "naturally," simply means that their ways (*daos*) of being/doing are not separate from but move as expressions of the Way (*Dao*).

For an elder, to learn one or more of these "ways" of being/doing can free him or her from the myriad external and internalized forces whose overriding goal has been to shape their "way" of life into a means of service to and reflection of society's wider economic, political and cultural interests and demands. And the elder **can** do it.

As Dr. Sherwin Nuland has stated:

> Man is the only animal to have been granted the ability to continue developing during the later periods of life, and much of this depends on seeing oneself as the kind of person who can overcome the tendency to do otherwise. It is incumbent on us to use this ability. (Nuland, 115)

We can be our own worst enemy, especially when we underestimate our power to make changes in our ways of knowing, being, and doing. Often we expect others to change things for us. Or we can easily blame "human nature" or make individualized excuses: "That's just how I am." Certainly, both human nature and our own selves are full of negative and positive possibilities. And, yes, we have developed habits and attitudes that work against the changes needed both to rediscover and rejuvenate our unique creative potentials and to find "ways" of performance that give release to and replenish our newly found sources of energy and wisdom. It might require dedicated persistence and "practice." But, as Nuland remarks, "No matter the difficulty, it is necessary to reach into the complex of interacting and competing impulses and instincts, to choose those that promise later years of [self] fulfillment and value to others" (Nuland,114). The two are interrelated as a dynamic dialectic within a reciprocating whole.

What are called the "skill stories" of Chuang Tzu demonstrate how seemingly unremarkable individuals can display holistic wisdom through the sensitive attention to the complex contours and sometimes dramatic, sometimes nuanced reactions of "the other." One can begin the transformation today. Nuland insists that "[t]he difficulties lessen with each small triumph after the first few." And as the difficulties lessen one moves closer toward being the kind of elder one aspires to be (Nuland,114). We need these small triumphs to boost our confidence and keep the process going. Often we must simply "drag our protesting selves kicking and screaming into action" (Nuland, 115).

Recent studies on aging and brain plasticity have demonstrated how important it is for older people to keep challenging themselves mentally. Although there may be some areas of inevitable decline, researchers are discovering that the brain can continue to grow and develop to compensate for losses. Its "plasticity" allows the brain to reform and reshape itself until the moment of death. Chuang Tzu introduces us to crafts persons and artisans--many of whom are elders--who develop their respective skills with such proficiency, grace and effectiveness that they are judged by many to possess supernatural powers. While it might seem that the crafts persons Chuang Tzu explores simply do the same things over and over again, as we shall see, this is a mistaken interpretation.

Operating within a cramped society that does not encourage the expansion of the human spirit, our conventional ways of knowing and doing were formed as ways of confining human aspirations and redirecting human potentials into the service of powerful institutions and individuals within society. Meant to spiritually fly, humans were told that crawling (sometimes over one another) was their vocation, although they were permitted their veneration of a few sages who could actually walk.

As we have seen, some Daoist "ways" begin with "forgetting," "fasting of the mind-heart," and other similar practices that help free mind-and-heart from oppressive mental, behavioral, and emotional traits and enable one to get back in touch with and reclaim innate potentials. In the words of Philip Ivanhoe, one learns to "keep in contact with one's innate tendencies and intuitions" so that one can "come to recognize the patterns and processes inherent in the world and learn to move in harmony with them" (Ivanhoe, 61).

Such practices also teach one how to "maintain the openness and flexibility needed to deal with novel situations and circumstances" (Ivanhoe, 61). This means developing both inner freedom and a mirror-like mind that sees/reflects things as they are and then responds to them from one's recovered and revitalized authentic self. Chuang Tzu presents us with a number of people who have embarked on and been transformed by an art or way (*dao*) to the point where their actions "flow out in spontaneous response to their illuminating perception of each situation" (Ivanhoe, 104).

Any number of "ways" can help cultivate as well as provide a graceful outlet for one's newly tapped potentials via a sequence of effortless, spontaneous actions that will support, coordinate and harmonize one's whole being with the flow of realty's patterns and processes. "Zhuangzi's skillful exemplars," Ivanhoe points out, "have cultivated forms of skillfulness that enable them to match up the Heavenly within them with the Heavenly outside of them" (Ivanhoe, 105). In other words, if one is fortunate and develops far along the path or way, one takes "mastery" to another level, one of mastery through non-mastery.

The "Masters" who make their appearance in Chuang Tzu's tales, parables, and puns, are often personally odd, located low on the social ladder and not often the type of craftsman or artist that people assume embody, display, and convey wisdom. But they do possess and are possessed by a crazy wisdom that fills and inspires their lives. The initial reactions by many people to their wise actions or "ways" may include open-mouthed awe, considerable head scratching mixed with chuckles. Let's start with a man who catches cicadas (tree crickets)!

I

Concentration: Catching Cicadas

In Chapter Nineteen, Confucius encounters an old hunchbacked man who could catch cicadas on the sticky end of a long pole as easily as if he were picking them up with his hands. Confucius asks whether he has a special trick or secret method. The hunchback says he has a "way." For months prior to the cicada season, he prepares by balancing balls on a stick. If he can balance two, he knows he will lose few cicadas; if he balances three, he'll lose only about one in ten, and if he balances five balls, he knows he will catch cicadas as effortlessly as grabbing them with his hand. His concentrated stance fits into the forest milieu. His body is positioned to resemble a "stump with twisted roots" (Mair, 176). His arms are made to look like the "branches of a withered tree." He stands absolutely still, fully concentrated and so empty of thoughts of monetary or other rewards that he would not swap the wings of a cicada for all of "the myriad things" in the universe. "How can I not succeed?" he asks Confucius (Mair, 177).

The cicada catcher becomes a part of the natural world, like the cicadas themselves. He positions his own hunchbacked body until it looks like a tree-stump with its branches "sticking" out. Unmoving, alert to movements, present to the moment, stilled of emotions and empty of motives, the hunchback waits like a coiled spring. He fits into his surroundings so well that, when a cicada passes just at the right place and time, the stick springs into the air and catches it. His spontaneous, effortless-effort springs from and unfolds under the guiding energy of *Tao* and in accord with the ways of the natural world that are also shaped and guided by the Way.

This is not something that most children and adults practice: being here in the now, fully alert yet totally relaxed, seemingly frozen in stillness yet warmed by deep energy ready to spontaneously explode in an instant when all variables meet. This type of open concentration also keeps the crazy flood of random or anxiety-provoking thoughts at bay. This is not an escape from life but an immersion into life and an "escape" from one's own demons—or society's. (Compare this skill with a modern way of "catching" crickets by going online and ordering a box or two of live crickets which you receive in a day or two—take much "skill"?)

The Taoist-tinged Confucius, after hearing from the humpback, passes on this wisdom to his disciples: "In exercising your will, do not let it be diverted; rather, concentrate your spirit. This is the lesson of the hunchback gentleman" (Mair, 177). Or one can say that when one's whole being is concentrated, the will follows its inspired guidance.

DONALD P. ST. JOHN

II

Wisdom: Transformation not Information

There are many ways (*daos*) into the Way (*Dao*) and many ways to move, flow, express one's self, etc. with the Way energizing and guiding you. Manifestations of Dao's non-doing (*wu wei*) fill the universe and can enter and fill an important part of one's own way of non-doing. Dao cannot be captured or transmitted in words and concepts. One comes to a knowledge of Dao through finding a way (dao) to encounter it in life and within one's self as part of Life. A way (dao) teaches us a series of movements through which we can experience a way of holistic knowing that moves us beyond words and concepts and enables us to engage Life in a mutually responsive way, a way of give-and-take, move and respond, sense and shift, like dancing with a responsive partner. The deepening knowledge of Dao experienced in and through a dao, yields a corresponding deepening of one's self-knowledge; indeed an uncovering and emergence of the presence of one's deeper being.

Chuang Tzu was able to awaken individuals from the daze in which their normal life existed and provide insights into how to awaken their wider, deeper, more conscious (not self-conscious) self and mode of being. His exemplars included archers, wheel-makers, butchers, and even, as we just witnessed, cicada catchers. He demonstrated how the ways and wisdom of his "sages" often incorporated the wise *daos* of animals, plants and insects. Some of the Chinese Kung Fu/gong fu forms have been modeled on the central movements and concentrated patterns of energy-release exhibited by animals such as the preying mantis, tiger, crane, and even the "dragon."

There are many ways for today's elders to develop and express their intuitive talents through drawing upon the arts such as music, painting, poetry, and dance. Likewise, they can pursue meditative and contemplative modes of knowing that deepen self-knowledge while increasing the moments when self- and-other explore cooperative modes of being and doing that are mutually spontaneous and fluid-like. These can revitalize and enrich elders on all levels, expanding their sense of self while sensitizing them to others and to the harmonious patterns of the life-world of which they all are a part. Elderhood invites us to realize a new stage in life, a deeper level of wisdom and a richer sense of personal fulfillment. How rare does the mass media even hint at this!

III

Hands: Another Source and Expression of Crazy Wisdom

In Chapter Thirteen of the *Chuang Tzu/Zhuangzi,* we meet a young sophisticated Duke named Huan, who "Sat under his canopy/ Reading his philosophy" (Merton, 82). Nearby an elder wheelwright is shaping wood into a wheel. The crafty wheelwright leaves his place, approaches the Duke, and inquires as to what he is reading.

"The words of the sages," the Duke replies. "Are the sages still alive?" asks Phien, the Wheelwright. "They are already dead," the Duke replies. The wheelwright claims that if that is the case for these ancients, then what the Duke is reading is only the "crap" they left behind. "Crap?" asks the Duke. Insulted and angry, he threatens to have Phien executed unless he can give a satisfactory reason for his effrontery—and immediately!

Phien calmly explains himself, starting with the general dynamics of wheel-making. He notes that if he wants the wheel to be round, the pressure of his chisel must be just right—not too heavy and not too light. A disciplined sensitivity and intuitive way of knowing must inform his hand's movement. "If I am neither careless nor hurried, I feel in my heart that my hand is succeeding. I cannot express it in words—there is an art in it" (Ware, 94). Words express and inform on a rational level, carrying intellectual meaning from one human to another or others. But they cannot capture the deeper pre-conceptual meaning that underlies and informs them and so much of life.

Phien confesses that he cannot tell his son how to do what he does and his son cannot learn it from him simply through the use of words. That is why he is still making wheels after seventy years. And that is also why the sages took what they really knew, the source of their words, with them to the grave. What they left behind were simply their droppings, and that is what the Duke is now reading. (Whether this satisfied the Duke is not noted by Chuang Tzu.)

Here the *Chuang Tzu* contrasts the "know-how" of Pien with the "know-that" or "know-about" of Huan. Pien's wisdom is experiential, direct and immediate while Huan's knowledge is conceptual and second-hand. Pien's wisdom cannot be abstracted from the living interaction between the craftsman and the wood. No "how-to" manual could adequately explain, even with detailed words, the kind of knowledge that can only be conveyed by holding the chisel, feeling the turning wheel, responding to the changing shape of the wood and at the same time building a mutually sophisticated relationship between heart and hand.

Pien's wisdom is the result of many sessions of intimate interaction with the "other" (wood and wheels). Such "know-how" only comes about through give-and-take, trial and error. Pien has to "feel" or "listen" to reality in an open, total way. Reality "speaks" to him in a unique way through each block of wood. He attentively responds to it, using the language of heart and hand. This series of "living" dialogues creates new truths that (respectfully) transform the wood and Pien.

A wise elder will see that this is not a result of muscle power and will power. Confucius said of the cicada master that the primary thing was to concentrate one's spirit (*shen*). The will is subordinate to it as a guiding and directing faculty. The wheelwright talks about the heart moving the hand. Also important is a sensitive feel for the changing contours of the "other." This "way," like most, integrates knowing, doing and being. Such per-formances are trans-formative. An elder engaged in learning the wisdom of one of these taos—elder-taos--which seem to be a simple art or craft will realize new personal possibilities within personal transformation. Of course the Chinese have developed the series of slow continuously flowing bodily movements found in T'ai chi ch'uan/taijiquan or the swifter moves in some of these like Kung Fu/gong fu. And whether in China or Japan (budo), these arts are not reserved to the young nor solely martial arts. The following passage by Zalman Schacter-Shalomi accentuates the positive influence of aging on this founder of the Japanese art of Aikido.

> George Leonard, author of *Mastery*, . . . believes that a spiritual practice when pursued on a regular basis can strengthen an elder's commitment to continued learning... Morihei Ueshiba, the founder of Aikido did not reach his peak as a martial artist until he was seventy years old. . . . Opponents who attacked him in ritual Aikido encounters typically described 'entering a cloud' and contacting a 'giant spring' that turned

DONALD P. ST. JOHN

them around and flung them through the air upside down. ...Morehei continued improving in old age, giving his most spectacular demonstrations in his eighties. (Schacter-Shalomi, 36-37)

Practice of these and similar disciplines or "ways," slowly educate, integrate and coordinate various levels of the elder, exciting them by an increase in their vital energy (*qi/ki*) and flexibility. And yes, "forgetting" also plays an important role in attaining the conscious yet embodied attention needed, as we shall see in the next story. The last thing one needs in the middle of one of these disciplines is a distracted or distracting mind.

IV

The Bell Carver: Fasting, Forgetting, and Seeing

In Chapter Nineteen of the *Chuang Tzu/Zhuangzi* we meet a craftsman named Ch'ing who had carved a bell stand of such mystery and beauty that everyone who saw it was amazed and convinced that it must be the work of spirits. The Marquis of Lu was likewise impressed and asked Ch'ing what his "art" might be. Ch'ing begged off, protesting that he was a mere craftsman not an artist and therefore could have no "art" (Watson, 126-7). But he did offer insight into what we might call the spiritual discipline of his craft.

Because he recognized the need to conserve and focus his vital energy (ch'i/qi), he began each project by fasting so as to calm and quiet his heart/mind (hsin/xin). After three days of fasting he forgot any concern with status and wealth. After five days he forgot any care for fame or blame, skill or clumsiness. After seven days he forgot he had a body or four limbs. Along the way, he had gradually forgotten the Duke himself and the Court. He was ready to focus all of his energy on his inner image of the bell stand, having eliminated all distractions from within and without (Watson, 127).

Only now could he enter the mountain forest and contemplate the inborn heavenly nature of the trees. At some point, as he gazed at the trees with open sensitivity, a particular tree's inner form or "heavenly nature" would reflect and resonate with the image of the bell stand within his own innate or heavenly nature. At that moment, he instinctively and spontaneously moved his hands forward to begin the carving. These steps were essential, for as he confessed to the Duke, if there had been no connection between his inner spirit (the heavenly pattern within) and the tree's inner spirit (heavenly pattern within), there would not be a bell stand. He suggests that perhaps it is this deep aesthetic-spiritual connection, now embodied in and shimmering out of the bell stand, that people sense when they claim that spirits were involved (Ibid).

The woodcarver moved to his more "mystical" level by disciplining his bodily appetites through fasting, clearing his mind/heart of desires for and thoughts of fame and ambition, and all the while becoming more centered and aware. Having forgotten the usual separation between self and other, he felt a resonance between Heaven within himself and Heaven within the tree.

"Heaven" for the ancient Chinese, claims Jullien, is "the full regime of natural processivity." For the bell carver it is "the refuge of his vitality" and makes him immune to external "elements and dangers." Instead of allowing fear to enter or arise within him and to become either paralyzed or moved to act prematurely, "he is moved by *processive* reactivity alone" (Jullien, 51). He achieves an integration of his whole being due to his immersion in and openness to the natural processivity of "Heaven" or *"Dao/Tao"*. As we saw, Chuang Tzu used the example of a drunk who, with his wholeness intact and hence lacking "affective reactivity," fell out of a speeding, bumpy wagon but was unharmed. Likewise, when the person of integral wholeness encounters the bumps and thumps of life he or she takes them in stride. As Jullien would phrase it, he or she is protected by *"natural* processivity alone," having lost their *affective* processivity (Jullien, 51).

The Bell Carver would no doubt agree that the saying, "spirit is empty and waits on all things," aptly describes what was happening as he waited for the manifestation of the bell stand in the tree. It seems clear that there is a Daoist path to a subtle transformation and "merging" of the physical, vital, conscious and spiritual (refined evergy *qi)* "levels" in such a way that one is able to identify and engage with similar levels present in the world. Thus the physical level of the person is filled with Life, Life with Consciousness, Consciousness or mind with Spirit or subtle *qi*. For elders this implies that when the many blocks to doing so vanish from the dynamic at work, and when they return to their true being, the result of opening to and allowing themselves to be guided by *incitement* (Jullien's rich term), and consequently to enter into "contact with a more intimate source of energy" (Jullien, 48). In this context, "feeling" and "touching" no longer refer only to physical acts and experiences, but to our permeation by and exercise of a deeper and "more intimate source of energy" (Jullien, 48). ("Spirit" is not to be understood in a dualistic spirit/matter context).

This more expansive experience lies behind the claim made by Cook/ Butcher Ding (whom we will discuss more fully in the next chapter) that he no longer "sees" with his eyes but with his spirit.

> My senses are idle. The spirit
> Free to work without plan
> Follows its own instinct. (Merton, 46)

Cook (or Butcher) Ding's declaration that his "spirit" sees and follows its own "instinct" while being guided by the Oxen's "natural line," suggests that he, like many other individuals in the "know-how" or "knack-stories" (Graham's fortuitous term), has attained on all levels a high degree of sensitivity and awareness that allows him to move in a spontaneous, harmonious manner. Artisans like the Bellcarver establish a vital integral rapport with other beings and the movement of the context within which he and they live and move and express their being.

So it can be with an elder who wishes to "carve" out a life. Limits are not a problem but an opportunity for him or her to apprehend deeply and act creatively, guided by life's moving inner spirit and that of the multitude of challenges and opportunities with which he or she is involved. New limitations brought on by the changes of life will arise but with them will also come opportunities for new creative responses. This type of "spirituality" is not an escape from life but a deeper and more flexible way to respond sensitively to and move fluidly with its changes. This transformed elder self will enable one to move with life's energies and patterns while at the same time maintaining one's inner balance through resting in one's still, empty center as we will see in the chapters on "transformations".

Daoists, and certainly Chuang Tzu, would say that many of our adult behavioral, emotional, and mental "skill patterns" are the result of educational and vocational training to prepare and shape us for economic and social positions in the dominant society. We have been told-or erroneously assumed- that many of the internalized patterns of social conditioning when displayed by us were adequate expressions of who we were and the growing reality of who we were to become. Chuang Tzu's challenge for the elder is to re-evaluate, reshape, or eliminate these—in a *wu wei* (non-assertive, spontaneous) sort of way. One can have access to more intimate individual energies (*qi)* and potentials that can be synchronized with and sensitively coordinated with those of the larger Life process.

This move into a more fulfilling and revitalizing way of being and doing will require self-examination and self-scrutiny so that we can recognize and activate our authentic potentials. As Sherwin Nuland wisely notes, elders are filled with "competing impulses and instincts" which means that those of us who desire to pursue authentic growth, must face the fact that "choice exists for each of us, though it may sometimes involve a deliberate and difficult overcoming of lifelong tendencies or patterns in the opposite direction" (Nuland, 115). But, when we do accept the challenge, and start making these difficult choices, we see that "the difficulties lessen with each small triumph after the first few . . ." (Ibid.). Fortunately, "[i]n the doing of these things we after a while begin to think of ourselves as the kind of people who do these things; we then do more of them" (Nuland, 114). The skills and ways of these exemplars in the *Chuang Tzu* as well as later versions of Chinese biospiritual movements and meditation practices can help an elder locate and develop his/her authentic potentials and leave incompatible impulses and habits to wither.

To respond to the new contours of elderhood, we cannot return to the confrontational, power- or ego-centered ways of adulthood. Adaptability, flexibility and creativity emerge with the elder's ability to spiritually and psychologically free himself or herself from goal-obsessed and economically defined patterns of behavior. Hence, the elder will make new choices supported both by inner energies (*ch'i/qi*) and enriching external movements. Moving with the flow requires a creative engagement with disciplines and "ways" that draw upon our best qualities as they incite and energize our emerging elder-self at all levels. New enlivening patterns and processes begin to unfold in our lives and we grow as we open to and cooperate with them.

As a result, our intact wholeness will help us weather and even glide upon the particular storms of the last phase of life. As embodied beings we can at the same time respond to and be guided by the energy and spirit permeating us. Hence we will be able to coordinate all appropriate "impulses and instincts" in a healthy way into the new art of our stage of living (Nuland,115). Whether sixty, seventy, eighty, ninety or one-hundred, an elder's *dao* (way) should allow him or her to renew their inner energies and skillfully use them both to sensitize themselves to and coordinate their actions with life's changing external and internal rhythms and energies.

WORKS CITED

Ivanhoe, Philip J. and Karen Leslie Carr. *The Sense of Antirationalism: The Religious Thought of Zhuangzi and Kierkegaard.* Lexington: Create Space Independent Publishing Platform, 2010.

Jullien, Francois. *Vital Nourishment: Departing from Happiness.* New York: Zone Books, 2007.

Mair, Victor H. *Wandering on the Way: Early Taoist Tales and Parables of Chuang Tzu.* New York: Bantam Books, 2004.

Merton, Thomas. *The Way of Chuang Tzu.* New York: New Directions Publishing Corp., 1965.

Nuland, Sherwin B. *The Art of Aging.* New York: Random House, 2007.

Schacter-Shalomi, Zalman. *From Age-ing to Sage-ing.* New York: Warner Books, 1995.

Watson, Burton. *Chuang Tzu: Basic Writings* New York: Columbia Univ. Press, 1964.

CHAPTER EIGHT

COOK TING/DING: A WAY FOR AN ELDER

I

Contemplative Movement, Holistic Awareness

Most of us have had the experience of "losing ourselves" while being totally absorbed in an intense action like dancing, playing music, even dribbling a basketball down court. In this kind of "flow" our *being* is not separate from our *doing*. There are "ways" in which who you are and what you do unite. In some cases, these (*taos/daos*) become "ways" in and through which the Way (*Tao/Dao*) can be experienced and expressed. Ironically it is by *wu wei* (non-doing) that the doer is most deeply enriched.

In the figure of the butcher and cook named Ting/Ding, Chuang Tzu/Zhuangzi gives us a special insight into the dynamics of a "way." Ding was another commoner who taught a nobleman a lesson about life. But, unlike Duke Huan in the wheelmaker story, Lord Wenhui in the story of Ding clearly "gets it." In fact, it is Wenhui who initiates a conversation with Ding after being stunned by the graceful rhythm and timing of the butcher's movements, which were

> Like a sacred dance,
> Like "The Mulberry Grove,"
> Like ancient harmonies! (Merton, 45)

The Prince loudly exclaims, "Good work!" and "Your method is faultless!" (Merton, 45). The butcher, laying aside his cleaver, replies: "Method?" ... "What I follow is Tao / Beyond all methods!" (Ibid.).

With these words, Cook Ding suggests that his "work" is something more than just another routine execution of a set of frequently repeated actions. A method is a standard operating procedure, a set way of doing things that can be mastered by almost anyone who follows the step-by-step instructions. A method is universally available and with repetition, mastered! If his secret isn't a proficient method or technique, what is it?

Cook Ding points to the changes that have occurred within him and their influence over the years on his way of "seeing" and relating to an ox. In the beginning, he only saw the ox as one solid mass; then he learned to see "the distinctions." Now he does not "see" with his eyes only but apprehends with his "whole being."

My senses are idle. The spirit

> Free to work without plan
> Follows its own instinct
> Guided by natural line,
> By the secret opening, the hidden space,
> My cleaver finds its own way.
> I cut through no joint, chop no bone. (Merton, 46)

The depth and subtlety of the butcher's "spiritual" perception can be inferred from the keenness of his blade. A good cook changes cleavers once a year ("he cuts"); a poor cook needs a new cleaver every month ("he hacks"). But Ding's cleaver has cut up thousands of oxen over a nineteen year period and "Its edge is as keen / As if newly sharpened" (Merton, 46).

According to Francois Jullien, a transformation on and to all levels of Ding's body, mind, and spirit gives birth "to a *subtle and unimpeded perception*" that transcends "the stage of the crude and tangible" and gives "access to 'subtlety'" and delves "into the invisible" (Jullien, 90). (I draw upon Francois Jullien's treatment of the Cook Ding story because it can be uniquely helpful for elders seeking "crazy wisdom").

This means, as the butcher says, that when he moves beyond the limited knowledge of the ox's reality provided by his senses, his "spiritual faculty seeks to go further by attending to the natural ["heavenly"] structure of the animal" (Jullien, 88). What had been initially perceived as simply an "object," and "a banal presence," now "enters into a partnership with the butcher's internal perception" (Jullien, 89). According to Jullien, this "deepened perception" now "reveals the ox relieved of its opacity (which had imposed its 'wholeness')"(Jullien, 90). Or, put another way, "[t]he ox has been opened up for him (as though X-rayed by spirit)" (Jullien, 90).

The refining or decanting of this internal power of perception, then, both refines the opacity of the ox and allows for contact with ("seeing") its internal, more subtle ("heavenly") structures, "just as the wood of the tree collaborates with the carpenter to create a bell stand" (Jullien, 90). In general, what is special about this "transcendent faculty of perception" is a type of ongoing, evolving "contact" which is sensitive to maintaining a "harmony with things" (Jullien, 90).

II

Tough Spots, Fluid Motion

Yet the harmony is not static or marked only by an endless, smooth flow. Neither one's relationship with life, nor one's relationship with an ox, are without "tough" spots, as the butcher admits:

'True, there are sometimes
Tough joints. I feel them coming,
I slow down, I watch closely,
Hold back, barely move the blade,
And whump! The part falls away
Landing like a clod of earth.' (Merton, 47)

Again it is with his whole being that he "feels" the tough joints coming. This is full attention, relaxed yet well-focused. He does not attack life's obstacles, nor does he avoid them; least of all, does he resort to a ready-made technique or one-size-fits-all plan labeled "how to deal with tough joints." If time allows, he has a sense for their emergence before they appear and he is able to more "intelligently" (not necessarily "cerebrally") deal with them. He slows down and is patient, watches closely, is attentive and self-controlled, yet primed to act when the time is appropriate.

> 'Then I withdraw the blade,
> I stand still
> And let the joy of the work
> Sink in.
> I clean the blade
> And put it away.' (Merton, 47)

Joy is a major component of this kind of experience. Similarly, there is an intrinsic satisfaction and joy that permeates musicians during a symphony or jazz work well-played, or dancers during a duet well-danced. One needs no extrinsic reward outside of the experience of the intrinsic value and joy of the work itself. The concentrated, absorbed state may last for many minutes. As with the cook, the spell is broken as the movement of limbs and trunk, the flow of the energy (*qi*) through body/cleaver ceases. The butcher separates his whole being from the ox by withdrawing the blade. The energies return to Ding and sink in, leaving a penetrating, circulating joy and contentment ("I stand still"). Chuang Tzu also mentions joy in relation to Heaven or Tao. In Chapter Thirteen he declares that Heaven's joy comes from, among other things, its "carving of all forms without any artful skill!" (Waltham/Legge, 159). How profound! And how important for humans as members of the Earth community to take it to heart, especially in this heavily technological world.

So Cook Ding withdraws from his carving and allows the joy of the work to sink in.

> Prince Wan Hui said,
> "This is it! My cook has shown me
> How I ought to live
> My own life!" (Merton, 47)

Or, as translated by Jullien: "Upon hearing the words of Butcher Ding, I understand what it means to feed one's life" (Jullien, 88-89). One truly "feeds" or nurtures one's life not by learning how to more forcefully dominate another or boost one's ego by learning to exert more power in order to control others, whether human or other-than-human beings, whether through money, technology, physical strength or narcissism. In the case of the Cook, he could not remain satisfied with his performance as a "hacker" even though that would have been enough for him to keep his "job." He practiced and developed not only his skills, but his whole approach to the ox until they were all harmoniously connected in an artistic performance that transcended any one of them: a whole greater than the sum of its parts. He never allowed himself to define excellence as an increase in efficiency or production rates or other measures of dominance. Bringing human life and its activities into a proper accord with the patterns of Nature (Heaven) is the Way of *Dao* and of *daos* and the way to "nurture" life, individually or communally. Forging human actions as an attack on Nature so that our species is separated from participation in the Earth's Way of Wisdom is not "crazy wisdom" but just crazy. And in the long run a self-destructive "way".

The personal transformation of Cook Ding himself was an important consequence of this *dao*/way. The self-conscious, de-liberate attitude and the forceful, rehearsed, and muscular strokes of the early years gave way to the self-less, spontaneous, sensitive, seemingly effortless performance of his later years. The transformative expansion of his own perceptual powers was reciprocally and intimately related to his changing relationship with the ox. The ox was now perceived with Ding's whole being and became an extension of himself and a part of a larger dance within the pattern of Heaven. If humankind-or- unkind would have moved historically, socially, economically, etc. according to this vision and way of being and doing, an ecologically-sound yet humankind-full world would exist. Elders who see themselves and fellow humans both as parts of a Whole and expressions of a single process would want to make strong objections to our present ecologically destructive actions and show a different "way."

And so, it is more accurate to say that the cook as a whole being who is in touch with Whole Being, consciously touches and is touched by the ox than to say that his mind directs his body in terms of the skill of butchering. Mind is sensitized by body and body permeated by mind. Both are embraced and moved by a subtle spiritualized energy. As the *Lieh Tzu* states:

"My body is in accord with my mind, my mind with my energies, my energies by my spirit, my spirit by Nothing." (Graham, 77). Given all of this, one can only conclude that the cook is a *ren shen* (spiritual person/ holy man).

III

Open to and Flowing With Change

How should an elder read this? How can he or she take it to heart and action? Must elders all become butchers? According to Francois Jullien,

> True comprehension cannot come until I have gradually incorporated into myself the ability to remain open to change. . . As the endless flowing gestures of Chinese gymnastics, (such as *taijiquan*) still teach today, this is the condition that must be satisfied if we are to remain sharp and resist being worn down, just like the butcher's knife after years and years of use. . . (Jullien, 92)

Spontaneity cannot occur at the beginning of practice. Any alleged spontaneity at that point would be simply an unruly release of feelings or impulses. The "instincts" that the butcher refers to are spiritual/aesthetic impulses (*shen yu*) that have emerged over time. A Mozart-lover with no technical skill cannot play Mozart, no matter how internally attuned to Mozart he or she is. On the other hand, a pianist with the requisite technical skill may be able to accurately play the notes Mozart put down on his score but not "play Mozart." Something else must be present, a Mozartian "spirit" that flows up and through the pianist, excites layers of aesthetic intelligence, fondles and strikes the keys to fill the air with the sound of Mozart's genius.

If Mozart is to play through you, as Tao played through the butcher, both excellent technique and spiritual sensitivity are needed--and something more. This "more" emerges when the two unite and it remains, keeping the two moving together. You are not a robot passively allowing some impersonal Mozart to "play" his music by pulling your strings. It is *your* performance, both as an interpreter of Mozart as well as an embodied expression of Mozart's "spirit" or "daemon." You are "being true" to Mozart but at the same time "being true" to your artistic self. Two great pianists can play Mozart, bring the spirit of the Master into the concert hall, but give differently nuanced performances. In fact, the same person may give two slightly different performances of the same Mozart sonata while filled with the spirit of Mozart. One cannot arbitrarily play or imitate another variation—that is to fall into ego consciousness, to lose Mozart.

What limits as well as propels all of this is the score. Mozart has written certain notes in a certain sequence with certain directions as to tempo or expression. Just as the ox provided a particular structural complex of bone, muscle, and tendons, so the written score presents its structural limits and demands (as does the piano). Yet, that which limits can also free. The butcher is totally concentrated yet totally relaxed; in control of his cleaver, yet not arbitrarily wielding it; responsive as well as anticipative. A sensual world both within and without (responding, receiving, enacting) lead to a still center from whence the energies ripple forth through mind/body with a flow forwards and a return to rest.

It is a world within another world. As T.S. Eliot expressed in *The Four Quartets,* language can only suggest this state through paradox, ". . . or music heard so deeply/That it is not heard at all, but you are the music/ While the music lasts." (Eliot, 44) Being wholly present allows one to adapt and respond to Reality as it presents itself, without conceptual impositions or moral judgments.

Cook Ding preaches Dao without using words. Like the wheelwright Phien/Pien, he is a Master of "wordless preaching." This teaching had its effect on the Prince who admitted that he had learned from Ding how to nurture and care for his own life. One element, as we have seen, was the open, sensitive, and integral Way of the Cook in responding to the demands of his craft. But this integrated unfolding in time and the unfolding of the "flow" were also essential in helping the Prince grasp the significance of what he has just "seen." In that way, as he had hinted earlier, Ding's performance resembled an extended dance and/ or musical tune.

The full "meaning" and subtle effect cannot be caught in one experience or one movement. Only as the work unfolds—if the composer knows her craft--does the element of "inevitability" grasp the audience and produce the "meaningful" experience. Cook Ding is both a composer and a performer, a jazz musician developing a theme and improvising on it, embracing limitations but not losing creativity. The Way un-folds and, yet, its inevitability is not predictability. The performance is as much creative as programmed, as much free as determined, for "you are the music while the music lasts." The performer, working with both what has been given and what he/she has to give, creates an integral work of art that is only meaningful and "inevitable" in hindsight.

Sometimes, as T.S. Eliot suggests, "We had the experience but missed the meaning. And approach to the meaning restores the experience/ In a different form beyond any meaning/ We can assign to happiness." (Eliot, 39) The meaning was there in the experience but it was not fully developed in our consciousness or life. One works with the limitations of space and time, with the limitations of body and mind. One slows down; one speeds up; one surveys and weighs, one acts and reacts. One suffers and rejoices even as one falls off of and climbs back again into the saddle on the Way. Nothing is extraneous; nothing unnecessary; all is inevitable yet unpredictable. The hacker becomes the cutter who becomes the artist. Meaning is sought in the historical past, present and future. Yet the Way, moving beneath, through and beyond all human centuries and years, saves, restores, accommodates, supports. How to join with it and jettison our narrowly human meters of meaning?

As T.S. Eliot wisely notes:

> Only by the form, the pattern,
> Can words or music reach
> The stillness, as a Chinese jar still
> Moves perpetually in its stillness. (Eliot,19)

Cook Ding moved in time, through time, and in a timely manner. His body parts moved in synchronic rhythm like a dance troupe or an orchestra whose sections played together. Yet there was a "silence," even amidst the music; and a "stillness," even within the movement. Neither the silence nor the stillness were simply the absence of sound or movement after the performance. Ding's "spirit" was present in the concentrated mind, the swinging arm, the planted foot, and to itself. To paraphrase Chuang Tzu: The Tao is always still, always at rest; and yet It does everything that is done.

The silence of the violin co-existed with the sound of the vibrating strings. And the pattern revealed in the unfolding of the performance was already in-folded at the beginning. But where? That which is infolded in the performer is unfolded in the performance. And so the performer is both an instrument and the performance: freedom, silence, stillness, and also form, sound, movement. The Dao both precedes the *de* and unfolds through the *de*.

The Art of Elder Life rests upon: 1) drawing meaning out of the "whole" of the life performance experienced so far, 2) being buoyed by the surge of its melody and movement, and 3) being nurtured by its silence and stillness. If the final movement is to bring to completion what the sequence of life events have been building towards, the elder must exercise a sensitivity to his life's major themes and to their direction so that a creative finale emerges, true both to the past works and the creativity still emerging from within. A "fitting" ending requires both a flowing towards the opening, an instrument that slides through it, and an opening through which the Cook moves all of his spiritual energies. Ding lets the joy of the work sink in. Is this the end, or the beginning, or both?

> Or say that the end precedes the beginning,
> And the end and the beginning were always there
> Before the beginning and the end. (Eliot, 19)

WORKS CITED

Jullien, Francois. *Vital Nourishment: Departing from Happiness.* New York: Zone Books, 2007.

Eliot, T.S. *The Four Quartets.* New York: Houghton, Mifflin, Harcourt, 1943

Graham, A.C. *The Book of Lieh-Tzu.* New York: Columbia University Press,1990.

Merton, Thomas. *The Way of Chuang Tzu.* New York: New Directions Publishing Corp., 1965.

Nuland, Sherwin B. *The Art of Aging.* New York: Random House, 2007.

Waltham, Clae, Editor and James Legge, translator. *Chuang Tzu: Genius of the Absurd.* New York: Ace Books, 1971.

CHAPTER NINE

Transformations: Chuang Tzu

One must face squarely the humbling fact that sometimes the Way of the universe may not coincide with one's individual preferences as a member of the human species. None of us is exempt from the changes, pleasant and painful, experienced within our lifetime or the great and universal cycle of life-and-death (the Great Transformation) of which our life itself is a part. Sagely elders continue to experience their intra-life changes, but are increasingly aware of the spatially larger and temporally deeper transformational processes of the universe.

I

Myriad Transformations

In Chapter Six, Chuang Tzu notes:

> We are especially happy when we chance to take on human form. What incalculable joy there is in these myriad transformations, such as human form, which never begin to reach a limit! . . . If people will emulate one who is good at being young and good at growing old, good at beginning and good at ending, how much more should they emulate that to which the myriad things are joined and upon which the unity of transformation depends! (Mair, 55)

In the same chapter he tells the story of four friends who strike an unusual bargain: "Whoever can take nonbeing as his head, life as his spine, and death as his buttocks, whoever knows the oneness of life and death, of existence and nonexistence, we shall be his friends" (Mair, 57-8).

Soon Master Yu, one of the four, falls ill (to say the least). Master Yu is presented by Chuang Tzu as a Job-like figure, having suffered severe and painful changes to his constitution. Master Ssu, another of the friends, goes to visit him. When Yu sees his close friend, he exclaims:

> I am so doubled up
> My guts are over my head;
> Upon my navel
> I rest my cheek;

My shoulders stand out
Beyond my neck;
My crown is an ulcer
Surveying the sky;
My body is chaos
But my mind is in order. (Merton, 62)

Master Ssu asks Yu whether he is discouraged. He replies that he is not, and that no matter what is done to him, he will make something of it. If his left arm is turned into a rooster he will "announce the dawn." If his right arm becomes a crossbow, he will "procure roast duck." And if his buttocks become wheels and his spirit turns into a horse he will hitch himself up and take a ride in his own wagon (Merton, 63).

In short, Master Yu (Sir Chariot) neither passively accepts nor actively rebels against his fate. For him, one condition is replaced by another; a normal left arm is replaced by a crossbow left arm. Yu neither pines for the previous condition nor curses the present one. Rather, he is *present* to each phase as it *presents* itself. He is neither a teacher nor a philosopher who hands out "feel good" advice or "wise" platitudes. Rather, having rooted himself in his deep center, he draws upon that creative, yet formless and "useless" dimension of himself. His spirit is not crushed. In fact, his reply carries with it signs of a transcendental humor that points to a deep inner freedom.

Master Yu suggests that the way he is dealing with the changes to his body is the way one should look at and deal with life itself:

> Besides, to get life is to be on time and to lose it is to be
> on course; be content with the time and settled on the
> course, and sadness and joy cannot find a way in. This

is what of old was called "being loose from the bonds"; and whoever cannot loose himself other things bind still tighter. And it is no new thing after all that creatures do not prevail against Heaven. What would be the point in hating it? (Graham, 88)

According to Michael Puett, the goal of cultivation for Chuang Tzu "is to liberate oneself by no longer focusing on things." Things cannot "overcome Heaven" (Puett, 254). In other words, it is Heaven or Heavenly Dao that governs and guides the process that is responsible for the comings and goings within life and to life itself. The fact is, writes Puett, that "all things will inevitably be transformed into other things. To bind oneself to any one thing (including one's human form), is to commit oneself to cycles of joy and sorrow; only by complying with this ceaseless transformative process can one avoid resentment," as Master Yu does (Puett, 254).

A similar attitude and vision are evidenced by Master Li when he visits Master Lai who had become very ill and is near death. The first thing he does is to chase away Lai's family members, stating: "Don't startle him while he transforms" (Graham, 88). Then, as Li leans against the doorway, he addresses Master Lai: "Wonderful, the process that fashions and transforms us! What is it going to turn you into, in what direction will it use you to go?" (Ibid.).

This reminds us of the four men's opening "bargain" that centers on developing an inner attitude, a state of mental "emptiness," where all the myriad beings and states of being, like spine and rump, are experienced as equal, interrelated, and complementary. One who maintains an open and free disposition can creatively flow with the cycles, embrace and let-go of a variety of beings and states of being. When the flow that gave you life brings death, go with it, but not like a stick passively floating on top of a stream.

The way in which Master Yu handled his sudden and shocking transformations offers an elder a lesson on how to deal with the many but usually less dramatic changes that he or she experiences. Master Yu could deal with these transformations because he had found a center (like the hub of a wheel) that allowed for both a unique perspective on and presence to life. At the open center, he accepted with equanimity the coming and going of states of mind and conditions of body, affairs of state and the state of each affair. Empty of "I", he did not identify himself with nor allow himself to be tied to one condition or another and thus felt no need to desperately hang onto a departing condition or to forcefully push away an arriving one.

However, one must not suppose that he was a fearful, repressed soul, holding himself back from any response. Rather, he was able to be fully present to reality in all of its variations. On one level he flowed, on another he touched a deep inner stillness that was at the same time a font of energy and spontaneity. When energy is not wasted on always fighting the self-defined disadvantages or clinging to the advantages of change, then wisdom and energy become available with which to creatively deal with one's fate.

II

Companions in Tao

In Chapter Six we meet three other men who become friends and "companions in Tao" when they realize that each of them could positively respond to questions such as, "Who can climb up to heaven and wander in the mists, roam the infinite, and forget life forever and forever?"

(Watson, 82). To "wander" and "forget" are, of course, Zhuangzian terms indicating a mental/spiritual state wherein one obtains freedom from the world of conventional perspectives and values. It is a state in which life and death are perceived as equal phases of one process, death follows life as winter follows summer.

Master Hu was the first of the three to die. Confucius learned of his death and sent his erstwhile disciple Tzu Kung to participate in the funeral ceremonies. Tzu Kung was shocked by what greeted him when he arrived. In the presence of their dead friend's body, one friend sang at the top of his lungs, while the other casually played a lute. This was totally out of place! Tzu Kung indignantly challenged them on their protocol. They looked at each other, laughed, and then sarcastically asked: "What does this man [a Confucianist] know about the meaning of ceremony?" (Watson, 82-83).

The friends of Master Hu not only omit all formal ceremonial behavior, they substitute informal, light-hearted singing and playing. Tzu Kung considers their actions to be highly disrespectful, uncouth, and irreverent. Tzu Kung is flustered and hurriedly returns to Confucius to share his dismay. "What sort of men are they, anyway?" he angrily and dismissively asks the Master (Watson, 83).

To the disciple's surprise, Confucius launches into a lengthy praise of the superior spirituality of these Taoists, regretting that he had sent Tzu Kung to participate in the funeral. He states that such men are free of normal social customs and ceremonies, are one with Tao, and figuratively can wander and float on the qi/ch'i of Heaven and Earth. They regard life and death equally, are "forgetting" and unheeding of their bodies. Half the time, they do not know whether they are alive or dead or which came first, life or death. Using colorful, hyperbolic language, Confucius tries to express something of the cosmic freedom of spirit and mind that these men exhibit and why they are not bound by human customs.

Tzu Kung asks that if this is the case, then why does his Master conform to the rites? Confucius sadly admits that he is being punished by Heaven. People should forget each other in Dao, like fish forget each other in water. They should not fill their relationships with all kinds of rituals and rules of behavior. Tzu Kung is obviously bothered by his Master's praise for people who seem to be on the fringe of society, who hold no position or title, and who receive little respect from the people who matter. Asked about such odd, liminal persons, Confucius replies that what appears odd in the eyes of men can be great in the eyes of Heaven; and those who, because of their highly acceptable social behavior, are praised by their fellow humans, are frequently of little worth when judged in the light of Heaven (Watson, 83-84). This would indeed be "Crazy Wisdom" for the Confucianist Tzu Kung!

The context for Tzu Kung's outrage was the importance to Confucians of the traditional manner of mourning the dead. These elaborate ceremonies of mourning, burial and remembrance served two purposes. First, they officially promoted the deceased to the sacred ranks of the ancestors; second, they provided a formal ritual by which the behavior and emotions of the mourners can be strictly regulated. Furthermore, filial piety, a key Confucian value or virtue, demands that children express and demonstrate their deep respect for their deceased parents through a flawless and dignified performance of these ceremonies. They could not claim to have "respect" for their parents without a proper external expression via the approved rituals (*li*). Without externally patterned *li*, claims to respect the deceased as parent, relative or friend were judged to be false.

Chuang Tzu is not criticizing common expressions of grief but rather the often pompous and excessively formal gyrations of professional Confucian mourners and mourning ceremonies. After all, Hu's two friends are engaged in their own version of a ceremony, albeit irritatingly jovial and informal compared to the Confucian model.

Confucianists also sought to extend the symbolic control they exercised in the social order into the natural order. The meaning of death and indeed the cosmic cycle of life-and-death were reduced to social and cultural phenomena that could be dealt with ritually. The deceased became ancestors and were integrated into an extended kinship system where they become more powerful in some ways than they were when alive. For Chuang Tzu's "Confucius," the spirituality of the friends allows them to "wander in the single breath of heaven and earth" (Watson, 83). Their "ritual" reflects this perspective, expresses their own freedom, and celebrates the wider implications of this freedom for their friend. Rather than deify the social identity of their now deceased friend and project it into the cosmos, they celebrate the cosmic expansion of his free mind. He has returned to a formless phase following the human form.

III

Spiritual Freedom Within Ritual Participation

If the previous story celebrated the free and iconoclastic spirit of two Daoists that allowed them to take life and death as part of the natural "seasons" of existence, the following story in Chapter Six asks the question whether one can maintain this independence from the usual ties of life and death and still participate in customary funerary rituals.

This is the story of Meng Sun, a Daoist who was considered by everyone to be the greatest mourner in the state of Lu, the ritual capital of ancient China.

Yet when his mother died he cried without tears, without distress in his heart or sorrow in his mind. Yen Hui, another close follower of Confucius was baffled at this. He complained to the Master and asked for guidance (Watson, 84).

Of course, Chuang Tzu's Confucius praises the higher knowledge and freedom of Meng Sun, and claims that by properly performing these ceremonies he did not compromise his superior inner qualities. He neither surrendered to the pressure of others nor to an emotional need to become famous as a ritualist. Nor was he overcome by grief while in the midst of ceremonies focused on the traumatic loss that others felt. Was he merely a cold manipulator; an actor pretending to be more? Perhaps the key to his ability to be a Daoist who was also unparalleled in his mournful performance of Confucian ritual was his deep inner peace and freedom joined to his vision of life and death which differed from the conventional view. In the context of the universal cycle of change and transformation, Meng Sun did not consider life superior to death. His free inner center allowed him to flow with the changes, neither desperately hanging onto the fleeing past nor overwhelmed by a desire for wealth, social influence or heavenly status in the future.

Confucius asks Yen Hui how he can be sure that we are not all living in a dream state? The past as remembered is not the past as once lived. Memory is to present awareness as a dream is to being awake, except that the act of remembering takes place in present awareness. He was aware of and present to events that have passed and are now only alive as memories. How did he know that his "awakeness" event would become a "dream"? Furthermore, even his present remembering of the past will itself become a memory in the future.

IV

Who Are We? What Do We Do About this Life-Death Cycle?

Chapter Twenty-two of the *Chuang Tzu* offers some extended reflections on the origin of the myriad ("10,000") things, and the cycle of life and death. One section in particular, cast as a conversation between Confucius and the Daoist philosopher Lao Tzu, author of the *Tao te Ching/daodejing*), provides an overview of at least one Daoist cosmological perspective (whether Chuang Tzu himself was the author of this section is a matter of debate).

Confucius asks Lao Tzu (Old Tan) about "the perfect Tao" (Palmer, 191) or as Graham translates it, "the utmost Way" (Graham, 132). Lao Tzu avoids the temptation to wax metaphysical and, instead, offers some advice on the kind of spiritual discipline one needs if one is to really "know." He advises Confucius to "cleanse and purify your heart through fasting and austerities, wash your spirit to make it clean and repress your knowledge. The Tao is profound and almost impossible to describe!" (Palmer, 191). At the conclusion of his little speech, Lao Tzu again advises Confucius to be silent, to cease disputations, for the

Tao is beyond hearing and speaking. In between, Lao Tzu presents an evolutionary view of the origin of things:

> The brightly shining is born from the deeply dark,
> that which is orderly is born from the formless;
> the spiritual is born from the Tao
> the roots of the body are born from the seminal essence;
> all forms of life give each other shape through birth.
> (Palmer, 191)

The Old Master then describes the evolution of beings (the shaped), including living beings, some born from wombs, some from eggs. Of these living things there "are no tracks behind them when they come" and no border over which they cross when they depart (Graham, 132).

After eloquently extolling the Cosmic Way as well as the profundity of the knowledge of those who follow that Way, Lao Tzu questions the way of the Gentleman taught by Confucius. He implies that it is pathetically narrow and human-centered and is dwarfed by the spatial and temporal influence of the true Way: "Unfathomably deep, like the ocean! Looming so high, ending but to begin again! By its cycles it measures out the myriad things without exception" (Graham,132). For Lao Tzu, everything that is or ever was, draws upon the Tao which never fails. He wonders how the way of the Gentleman could exceed that?

Lao Tzu then invites Confucius to place human life in a proper perspective, one that clearly sees how brief an individual human life is when compared to the course of cosmic evolution. But, honestly facing this contrast should not lead to despair. Rather, it should inspire a person to sink into the most profound depths of his own being, the depths where he finds the Ancestor of all beings. Lao Tzu asks

Confucius to imagine one human being "balanced between yin and yang, dwelling between Heaven and Earth" (Palmer, 190). Viewed from this larger perspective of origins, "when life begins for him, he is just a collection of breath" (Palmer, 190). And, "though some die early or late, how much time is there between them? It is a matter of an instant" (Graham, 133). Life is short--whether one dies young or at a very advanced age.

Thus the elder who follows Old Tan's wisdom, would make herself present to the changing patterns and relationships of life, moving into and along with each as it arises but not hanging on to it as it departs. Her inbuilt nature or character (*hsing*) enables her to be attuned to situations and relationships; her Way is to respond to them at a deep level of inter-communion. In this way she emerges into fullness as did the legendary saints and sages of yore.

"Man's life between heaven and earth," Lao Tzu continues dramatically, "is like a white colt passing a chink [crack] in a wall, in a moment it is gone" (Graham, 133). For Lao Tzu, this all means that, "In a gush, a rush, everything issues from there; melting, merging, everything enters there. By a transformation you are born, by another you die; all that lives feels the sadness of it, man mourns over it" (Graham, 133).

Those of us who have experienced walking through old cemeteries can resonate with Old Tan here. One tombstone may note that a person died in 1820 at age 20, another that its occupant died in 1860 at age 60. From the perspective of one living in the twenty-first century, the span between the two deaths--or even since the two deaths--seems brief, seems to have vanished in a moment, like the racing white colt glimpsed through a crack in a wall. Lao Tzu does not ignore that humans mourn these passages. But he offers a perspective and invites us, even as we transform along with all of the myriad things, to enter into ourselves more deeply so as to experience the Ancestor, the Reality dynamically present in the cycles and transformations of the myriad forms.

For Chuang Tzu, dying is a *changing* that should also be a *yielding* to the Great Return. The Shapeless and Formless gave us shape and form and indwells as a unique energetic potential that is our individual nature. At some point every living being with shape returns to the shapeless. The wise elder who in his/her depths experiences this Reality has no need to argue about it or to try to prove its existence or spin philosophical theories about it. Of course, words and symbols are not totally useless. Yet, they do not yield the kind or level of knowledge that is needed to truly experience and directly grasp this deeper truth. As Old Tan says, "Better than disputation, silence." In silence we can grasp It "absolutely" (Graham, 133). Crazy (Contemplative) Wisdom.

VI

At Chuang Tzu's Death Bed

As we have seen, Chuang Tzu displays little sympathy for humankind's arrogant claim to superiority over all other beings as well as to its desperate attempt to escape, through every means possible, the interconnections and transformations common to all, but especially to animate beings. Like the author of Ecclesiastes, Chuang Tzu reminds us that there is a season for everything, that both life and death are part of the natural cycle. There should be no prolonged mourning period or elaborate funeral rituals, like the Confucians prescribed above.

In Chapter Thirty-Two, Chuang Tzu teaches this lesson when the time comes for his own death. Seeing that their master is dying, his disciples make plans for an elaborate funeral, from decorating his coffin and filling it with rare stones and jewels to surrounding him with mourners. But Chuang Tzu places his death and its symbolism into a cosmic context:

> I shall have heaven and earth for my coffin; the sun and moon will be the jade symbols hanging by my side; planets and constellations will shine as jewels all around me, and all beings will be present as mourners at the wake. What more is needed? Everything is amply taken care of! (Merton, 156)

The upset disciples complain to their Master that if his body would be left to lie out on the ground he might be eaten by "crows and kites." Chuang Tzu responds, "above ground I shall be eaten by crows and kites, below it by ants and worms. In either case I shall be eaten. Why are you so partial to birds?" (Merton, 156).

WORKS CITED

Graham, A.C. tr. *Chuang Tzu: The Inner Chapters*. Indianapolis: Hackett Publ. Co., 2001.

Mair, Victor H., tr. *Wandering on the Way: Early Taoist Tales and Parables of Chuang Tzu*. New York: Bantam Books, 1994.

Merton, Thomas. *The Way of Chuang Tzu*. New York: New Directions Publishing Corp., 1965.

Palmer, Martin, tr et.al. *The Book of Chuang Tzu*. New York: Penguin Arkana, 1996.

Puett, Michael J. "'Nothing Can Overcome Heaven': The Notion of Spirit in the *Zhuangzi.*" In *Hiding the World in the World,* ed., Scott Cook. Albany: SUNY Press, 2003, pp. 248-262.

Watson, Burton, tr. *Chuang Tzu: Basic Writings*. New York: Columbia University Press, 1964.

CHAPTER TEN

Transformations: Lieh Tzu/Lizi

I

Death: A Return to Where We Set Out From

Chapter One of the *Lieh Tzu* introduces us to the crazy wisdom of an elder named Lin Lei who was nearly one hundred years old. He wore a fur coat in the spring as he earned his food by picking up the grain dropped by reapers. But, contrary to expectations, he was constantly singing as he stooped and bent and worked his way through the fields. Confucius, always cognizant of the wisdom of elders, said to his disciples: "That old man should be worth talking to. Someone should go and find out what he has to say" (Graham, 24). (Let us pause and admire Confucius. How often does it happen in our society that someone, upon seeing an old person, say, a woman, ever thinks, "That old woman should be worth talking to"? The latter statement is most often reserved for a young woman but the man's advance is not made in pursuit of her wisdom!)

Tzu Kung, Confucius' most devoted disciple and one always anxious to please, asks if he can go and talk to Lin Lei. Tzu Kung approaches the old man and sighs, feigning pity and concern. He asks him not once, but several times, if he has any regrets—having ended up this way. Lin Lei asks why he should have regrets. Tzu Kung, not always the sensitive one, reminds him that when he was a child he never learned to behave, and that when he was an adult he never strove to be a success. On top of that, he had never married. Hence he has no wife or sons as he draws closer to death. In short, what possible reason could he have for being happy? Why is he singing? (Graham, 24-25).

Lin Lei states that he is happy—and for the very reasons that Tzu Kung thinks he should be unhappy. He has lived such a long life precisely *because* he "took no pains" to learn to behave and because he didn't struggle to be a success. Furthermore, if he is so happy now it is because he has no wife or sons to worry about in his old age. And above all, he is happy because death is near! A confused Tzu Kung protests that all people hate death and desire a long life. "Why should you be happy to die?" (Graham, 25).

Lin Lei, like Confucius suspected, did have something to say. He begins with a basic philosophical assumption: "Death is a return to where we set out from when we were born." And so, if he dies here could he not be born somewhere else? And. for Lin Lei, our belief that either life or death is better than the other cannot be verified. Could it not, then, be foolish to hang onto life so desperately? Maybe "present death" would be superior to "past life" (Graham, 25).

Tzu Kung is baffled and returns to Confucius to seek guidance on what Lin Lei said. Confucius reminds him that he had a hunch that the old man would be worth speaking to, and that proved true. Yet, Confucius expresses a little disappointment at the old man's response, claiming that while, indeed, he was a man who had "found it," he had not "found all of it" (Graham, 25).

What did this Taoist-like Confucius mean? Lieh Tzu suggests that Confucius was disappointed that Lin Lei still clung to the fantasy that the self that he now experiences while alive would be the same self that would "exist" after death, and furthermore that it might be happier than it is now. While the old man was smart enough to challenge the ordinary notion that life is more desirable than death, he did so by consoling himself with images of a happier state after death. He both raises doubts ("how do you know?") with one hand as he finds a way to lessen the fear of death with the other.

Confucius (as portrayed by Lieh Tzu) is suggesting that to completely lose the aversion to the thought of death one must lose one's attachment to life both in body and mind. If the old man had "all of it" he would treat life and death as equal realities. The hold that life naturally has on one's body is stronger than the hold an imagined reality has on one's mind. One experiences life and imagines death: the image itself causes a fear of death and, in reaction, one then imagines life being born from death. Instead of treating life and death as equal, Lin Lei imagines that "present death" will be better than "past life." This is the clue for Confucius that Lin Lei does not yet have "all of it."

As Lieh Tzu would state elsewhere in the same chapter, "the living do not know what it is like to be dead, the dead do not know what it is like to be alive" (Graham, 29). The old man, however, held that each does know the other. But, for Lieh Tzu, "[c]oming, we do not know those who went before, going we shall not know those who come after" (Ibid.). Here Lieh Tzu makes what should be a commonsense observation: we emerge out of the stream onto the surface not having known the myriad of other surface beings who had emerged from and sunk back into the stream during the long and multiple ages before us. We can only imagine who they were and what things were like for them. Likewise, what we know is incomparable to what we do not know just as the life we live is miniscule compared to what has gone before us. But why do we reject this commonsense knowledge about the past when it pertains to a future that will exist for endless ages after us? Surely it is also true that "going we shall not know those who come after" (Ibid.).

II

Whose Life is it Anyway?

Both the *Zhuangzi/Chuang Tzu* and the *Lizi/Lieh Tzu* record a conversation between Emperor Shun, the legendary pre-dynastic sage-ruler, and a subordinate minister (named Ch'eng by Chuang Tzu) who seems to have been a Daoist/Taoist. Shun asks the minister: "Can one succeed in possessing the Way?" The minister replies: "Your own body is not your possession, how can you ever possess the Way?" Shun retorts "If my own body is not mine, whose is it?" (Graham,29). In the *Lieh Tzu* we find the minister replying that one's body is a particular form lent "by heaven and earth." So with "life." We do not possess it. Rather, it is a "harmony" between our forces "granted for a time by heaven and earth." Nor are one's "nature and destiny" one's possessions. They "are a course laid down for you by heaven and earth" (Ibid.). In short, we are "the breath of heaven and earth which goes to and fro;" how can we possess it? (Graham, 30).

Our bodies and our lives are gifts and trusts that, after they have run their course, return to their true "possessor." In modern society, accumulating possessions is purportedly central to social status, self-image and even power. Perhaps the reality, however, is closer to what sages like St. Francis and Lieh Tzu knew: "I" can be possessed by my possessions. People who would consider themselves too sophisticated to believe in "spirit-possession" blissfully ignore their own "material-possession." While the idea of possession by spirits elicits laughter, possession by commodities elicits admiration. If I am possessed by my possessions then am I still a consumer or the consumed? Am I given worth by and because of my "things"?

Contrary to all of this, Lieh Tzu and other Taoists would hold that the Way of the Elder is the way of freedom, one manifestation of which is non-possession. This is not to be mistaken with the act of dis-possession. Rather, it is a mode of embodied presence wherein the "I" sinks into the intimate and self-renewing exchange of energy and consciousness between body and mind. Crucial to this shift is the "letting-go" of one's self as "owner" of mind and body and "consumer" of their respective pleasures.

Another manifestation of this freedom is experienced in travelling without knowing where we are going and staying in place without clinging onto it. In other words, if you are moving on the road, meaningful walking does not consist in having a clear idea of "your" destination and then smartly marching towards it, measuring distance travelled and yet to travel. If you decide to stay in one place, meaning and value do not come from making it into "your" place. The joy is: 1) to find a free way that allows you to wander without being obsessed with reaching some end point, 2) to settle into a place without "clinging" to it, and 3) to "dwell in" your body without possessing it. Not clinging to body or to place or taste, one is free to *be* and to "wander."

The statement "I am walking to get to X" becomes "I am walking," which now becomes "I am also being walked." When we say, "I am walking the dog," we are not denying that the dog is actually walking itself. What we mean to say is something like, "The dog's walking itself is a part of a larger context in which it is also being walked." If the dog could speak it might say, "I am being walked as I walk." This of course is only an analogy. Opening to the sense of being a part of a larger whole, a Daoist might say that "I am living my life while being lived by Life or Dao." Or, "I am being lived as I am living my life." Life as participation, inspiration (in-spiring), and co-creation (creative). My being is a participation in Being. Being moves and Becomes, in through, and with me. Its return to Non-being is also in, through and with/by me. I do not own my being; I did not create or cause my being.

Lieh Tzu's is a vision and a spirituality that de-centers the self as owner, possessor, and controller and places mind and body and energy/breath within the living breathing Being/Becoming of Dao within Nature. One is as much lived-through and breathed-by as one lives and breathes. Elders who desperately seek to hide or deny the movement of Life, close themselves off from access to a deeper identity and seek to reside instead inside of a small cramped "space."

How does one begin the transformation? A first step might be found in Lieh Tzu's counsel:

> Best be still, best be empty.
> In stillness and emptiness, we find where to abide;
> Consuming and producing, we lose the place.
> (Graham, 27)

Coming home to one's real abode requires: 1) a *giving up* of the possessive stance towards life that turns bonds of communion into chains of control, 2) an *opening up* that accepts vulnerability and mortality but also finds happiness in the simple gift of body, world, and others, and 3) a *waking up* to the present, to the wonder of picking up grain or washing dishes.

III

Awareness of the Flowing and Shifting of Time

A certain Yu Hsiang is quoted by Lieh Tzu:

> 'Turning without end
> Heaven and earth shift secretly.
> Who is aware of it?' (Graham, 27)

Lieh Tzu comments that: "Shrinking and swelling, maturing and decaying, it is being born at the same time that it is dying. The interval between the coming and going is imperceptible; who is aware of it?" He applies this to human life:

It is the same with a man's progress from birth to old age; his looks, knowledge and bearing differ from one day to the next, his skin and nails and hair are growing at the same time as they are falling out. They do not stop as they were in childhood without changing. We cannot be aware of these "intervals" but only of the effect over time. (Graham, 27)

Elders often remark: "How time flies! Where did it all go?" But even though quantitatively more time has passed between childhood and age 85 than childhood and age 65, experientially it often seems as if the same amount of time has flown by. Since our awareness is not coordinated with the subtle sequence of changes in body and mind, the seemingly constant flow of water underneath carries our boat further downstream. We experience the gentle undulation but do not take notice of the passing shore. And then we "wake up" for an instant when the younger crowd--of whom we still consider ourselves a part---identify us as members of the old group.

Those in their 50s judge that those who die in their 20s have had a short life, while those in their 80s consider those who die in their 50s to have been cheated. The Redwood tree sees the longest human life as short, but from the point of view of evolution's timeframe a Redwood is a recent phenomenon. For most Taoists, one should live in such a way as to die in one's natural time. Obstructing that flow can be the result of one's own actions or outside forces.

The sage, however, not only lives the flow of his or her own life, but sees beginning and end, life and death, as equally real, equally necessary, equally to be affirmed.

Lieh Tzu tells of a neurotic man so worried that Heaven and Earth might collapse, and, therefore, that "his body would have no place to lodge, that he forgot to eat and sleep" (Graham, 27-28). A friend, concerned about the anxious man, sought to enlighten him and lift his spirits. He patiently laid out all of the reasons why it is ridiculous to worry about heaven falling and earth crumbling. The worried friend's mind was pacified and both men were happy again.

Ch'ang-lu-tzu heard the story and smiled. He knew that in some ways no matter how light the air of heaven, or how heavy the metals of earth, both change and both will eventually perish. While this might not occur until far into the future, people who will be around near the time of that catastrophe should indeed worry. Master Chang-lu-tzu realized that the friend's well-intentioned response trivialized the worried man's concerns and ignored what might have been a prescient insight, to wit, that possibly even heaven and earth would someday perish. Hence, it is not inappropriate to worry about where the body or self would find support at that time (Graham, 28-29).

Upon hearing of this, Lieh Tzu smiled but added: "It is nonsense to say either that heaven and earth will perish or that they will not. . .we can never know." It is similar to the fact that neither the living know what it is like to be dead nor the dead, to be alive. "Coming, we do not know those who went before, going we shall not know those who come after" (Graham, 29). Even Chang–lu-tzu's wisdom turned out to be a projection by the living (who will be dead) of their own hopes and fears onto those who will be alive then. Lieh Tzu further argues that there is no need to worry about the body finding "support" if heaven and earth collapse. The body is interconnected with all other beings and is constituted by the combined forces of heaven and earth. If heaven and earth perish, the body will perish with them. No-body will be there to worry about the body finding or losing support. In the present time everyone feels supported and embraced by heaven and earth. Hence if one imagines a time when heaven falls and earth crumbles, one's self pictured living then is the same as one's self living now, and hence one is frightened by the possibility of the vanishing of all support. But can that be a concern of people who themselves vanish with the disappearance of heaven and earth?

Now if we interpret this parable as an existential tale about the fear of dying, we realize that Lieh Tzu is reiterating what Chuang Tzu had said: one must be a butterfly when one is a butterfly and be Chuang Tzu when one is Chuang Tzu. Since the word "body" can sometimes signify "self" the analogy is clear. Death threatens the self, the collapse of our World tears away support for the self or the "I." Chaos, death, and the void surround the solid "I" which once was supported by being and life. Where will "I" "be" at that time in that state? I am scared because I am thinking about the terror, fear and trembling that "I" will feel then. Yet as the World unravels, "I" unravel as well and by the time of the complete deterioration whomever is there will not be "I." Will there be an awakening?

The major context within which we should place our understanding of individual death in most of Lieh Tzu and Chuang Tzu is that of a transformative process of change that moves through and within all of the interconnected beings that have existed, exist and will exist. This includes Heaven and Earth. Graham himself explains that, in general, their Taoism holds that "there is no absolute difference between one thing and another, and encourages us to see death, not as the end of an individual, but as part of a universal process of transformation" (Graham, *Note*, p.22).

IV

Stealing from Nature ?

In the *Lieh Tzu* an intriguing discussion takes place between a poor man named Hsiang and a rich man called Kuo. The poor man, desiring to be rich, wants to know what the rich man is "good at" since he is very wealthy. The rich man boasts, "I am good at stealing" (Graham, 30). He admits that at first his stealing was amateurish and he could only provide for himself. Soon, and with practice, his stealing enabled him to support a large family. With time his stealing was so expertly efficient that he became the benefactor of his whole village. Hsiang was deeply impressed and inspired. Deciding on a career change, he became a thief. Unfortunately, after some initial success and a small accumulation of goods, he was caught and he lost everything. He went back to the rich man and complained that he had been misled. The rich man disagreed, saying that the poor man did not understand "the true Way of stealing" (Graham, 30).

Kuo then proceeded to give Hsiang a new perspective.

> I have heard it said: 'Heaven has its seasons; earth has its benefits.' I rob heaven and earth of their seasonal benefits . . . birds and animals, fish and turtles, are all begotten from heaven, and how can they become my possessions? Yet I suffer no retribution for robbing heaven.
>
> (Graham, 30-31)

"Commodities" on the other hand are produced, consumed or hoarded by humans. They are not products provided by Heaven. If you steal them, Kuo insists, you should feel guilty. Hsiang is not fully satisfied and relates the story to Master Tung-kuo. As a Master he digs deeper into the matter, asking Hsiang: "Is not your very body stolen?" This question brings us back to the earlier reflections on "possessing" one's own body. Since your very body is stolen, the Master continues, how can you not be stealing when you take food and other resources from the world in order to survive? (In other words, Kuo was not wrong in claiming to be a thief). Then, in an ecologically significant insight, the Master notes that every being under heaven and on earth is connected to every other being. It is a vast community. When we take from the earth community to sustain our bodies, what we take necessarily comes from or is another being or beings. However, this kind of stealing is "common to all" and hence there is no punishment or retribution. Kuo's "motive" for stealing, on the other hand, was "private" and he was rightly found guilty.

Master Tung-kuo goes one step further, noting that, "Whether or not you distinguish between common and private, you are still stealing. It is the power of heaven and earth that makes the common common, and the private private. For the man who understands the power of heaven and earth, what is stealing and what is not stealing?" (Graham, 31).

One might say that, today, humans are indeed experiencing "retribution" from the earth for excessively stealing and plundering its treasures. As a richly varied and sacred "gift," the earth and the universe (heaven) have not been appreciated by humans but considered their rightful "possession." Beginning with the belief that our bodies and lives are "goods" that we possess, we extend this claim to ownership to the earth body—and eventually perhaps to the heavenly bodies.

How would Master Kung-tuo characterize our use of Nature in the 21st century? In his terms, the private has taken over the common. No longer willing to hold the earth in "common" with other living beings, we claim it as our own. All is "private" or potentially so. Few still hold a reverential and thankful attitude towards Nature and its Source as giver of gifts. Ours is an anthropocentric vision of the universe and particularly of the earth. We do not recognize our common rights but enthrone the unfettered pursuit of private gain whether at the expense of nature or of the poor.

One notes in the story that Master Tung-kuo does not leave the rich man off the hook. But the wealthy man seems to have made his wealth through farming and used it to support his whole village. It was not simply a "private" motive nor was it so disruptive of nature that it destroyed "the commons." The web of life, the co-relatedness of the 10,000 things that Master Tung Kuo alluded to, the pattern that runs through the constantly moving and flowing Life process are in increasing danger of collapse. The cult of possessiveness and consumption, of the "private motive" as applied to multi-million dollar corporations are incompatible with the *Dao* of the Elder. The latter rejects the extension of the possessive ownership of *my body* to the possessive ownership of the *earth body* just as it balks from extending the possession of *my* life to the life and bodies of future generations (whether biological or cultural). And similarly, while we would condemn any "I" who poisons or kills *its* body, we rarely condemn the poisoning and eventual killing of an Earth-Body by our species which claims it as its own. This goes far beyond the distinction between common and private. Part of the grand illusion of modernity is that we have it all nailed down: what success is, what failure is, what bad luck is and what good fortune is.

Elsewhere, in Chapter 8 of the *Lieh Tzu*, we find two short tales that touch upon the themes of this environmental ethic. In the first we are informed that on New Year's morning the people of Han-tan presented a drove of living doves to their Minister. He was overjoyed and thankful and rewarded them. When asked by a visitor why the Minister did that he was told that their release as living beings was "a gesture of kindness" to them and one assumes the Earth. The visitor pointed out that the people compete with each other to catch the doves and in the process many doves are killed. "If you wish to keep them alive," says the visitor," it would be better to forbid the people to catch them." As it is now, the kindness in releasing them "does not make up for the mistake" of encouraging an action that brings them a reward but also in fact kills many. The Minister ponders this and says to the visitor, 'You are right.' (Ibid.).

The second story is quite enlightening. An aristocrat T'ien of Ch'i prior to setting out on a journey offered a sacrifice to "the god of the roads" and threw a huge banquet to say goodbye to scores of friends and followers. Looking at the fish and geese that his guests were being served, he reminded them to be grateful to Heaven which grows the "grains" and "breeds" animals, birds and fish "for the use of man" (Graham, 178). It was not an adult but a twelve year old boy who challenged this claim. He reminded all of them that the ten thousand things are born and reproduce like humans and "do not differ from us in kind" (Graham, 179). None of the 10,000 things is "nobler" (of more intrinsic value) than another although it might be more strong or clever (Graham, 178).

The boy reminds them that the world is filled with eaters and the eaten. But those who are eaten are not bred for that by heaven and this includes those eaten by humans. The youngster cleverly points out that "mosquitoes and gnats bite our skin, tigers and wolves eat our flesh; did heaven originally breed man for the sake of mosquitoes and gnats, and his flesh for the sake of tigers and wolves?" (Graham, 179). This perceptive and Taoist comment by the boy can launch us back into the present where the recent worldwide protests against the forces behind climate change and the deterioration of living beings and their habitats were led by young people like Greta Thunberg, a Swedish teenager.

V

Relative to Context and Free from Absolutes

Let us end with a famous Chinese tale in which a wise elder farmer teaches others some lessons about their quick and easy judgments about what is good luck and bad luck. This story comes in many forms but with the same message. I have created my version.

> Once upon a time there was an old farmer who lived with his son in an abandoned fort on the top of a hill. Obviously he was not wealthy or else why live in an abandoned fort? Yet, he enjoyed life, enjoyed his son, and managed to "get by" as we say. One day, however, he lost his only horse. His neighbors felt sorry for him and came by to commiserate with him on his bad luck. "Bad luck? Maybe," said the old man. A couple of days later, the lost horse found its way home, and lo! it had several wild horses with it. Immediately the neighbors came over to congratulate the old man on his good luck. "Good luck?" said the Elder, "we'll see." Soon his son decided to break-in one of the wild horses so he could have fun riding it. One day the horse threw the boy who broke his leg. Neighbors, hearing of the accident, came

by to express their sympathy at this bad luck. "Bad luck? Maybe not" said the old man. Not long after, war broke out and the recruiters came looking for young men and found a number among the old man's neighbors. But the old man's son could not walk and was of no use to the army. (My Rendering)

Each of these events was met with an instant judgment by the old man's neighbors. Aside from the intellectual pleasure it gives to know with surety what events in life count as "good luck" and which as "bad luck," there is the emotional reaction connected with joy and sorrow. Most people seek to assure good fortune and avoid bad luck, seek success and avoid failure. When failure comes, they are distraught, broken hearted, and disillusioned with life or perhaps disappointed in and angry with themselves or others. One sees similar reactions when an accident or a serious illness occurs. While there definitely are unequivocally "bad" things that occur, most events carry enough ambiguity with them that judgments about them should be viewed as tentative if not short-sighted. The judgments of the neighbors were both.

What proved them wrong was time and the often unpredictable and complex chain of events that can unfold from any single happening. Not only is immediate context important, historical setting is essential. Yet, who of us if locked into a perspective that judges all events in terms of "self-interest" can appreciate either or have the patience and wisdom to suspend judgment?

Elders should know better. Looking back over the course of a lifetime, do we not see many instances of bad becoming good and good becoming bad, of hasty judgments and quick emotional responses that we later regretted or were relieved to see as unrealistic? This ancient Chinese folk tale does not carry the message "Look for the silver lining" but "quit looking for linings, silver or black." Long-term happiness comes from long-term attitudes and perspectives. In the short-run it comes from an inner relaxed state, an ability to flow with events without grandiose exaggerations.

The tale is also telling us that life is a mix of bad and good events and "happenings," sometimes turning into each other, sometimes just being what they are. If we are free from the need for a godlike judgment on events, we can then respond in a variety of ways, or not respond at all. Do we really have to have an opinion on everything? Does our opinion matter that much in the scheme of things?

An event occurs and one group complains while another rejoices. Then the "tables are turned" and the reverse occurs. "I told you so" or "damn it," each group says at one time or the other. And yet, the (often political) melodrama goes on with the over-acting and emotional bloodletting. Wars are fought, won and lost. Thousands and perhaps millions die and then sides are shifted, alliances broken and made, enemies are friends and friends now enemies. At the very least, elders should raise their hands in caution and lower their voices. "Take it easy." "Let's wait and see." "Take your time." "Think it over." "Let's look at this from another point of view" or "in a different context."

And, in our own lives, we should be able to hang loose and look for alternatives, for unsuspected opportunities among the myriad let-downs. There are many possible storylines that could connect all or a series of events in our lives. And there are the ironies of life, the twists and turns, roads taken and not taken. Did the road not taken make all of the difference? Maybe. Remember that taking it might have been for good or ill or a mix. But even if taken, that road would have led to others—some taken and some not taken.

WORKS CITED

Graham, A.C., *The Book of Lieh-Tzu*. New York: Columbia University Press, 1990.

CHAPTER ELEVEN

Thomas Merton and Chuang Tzu's Wisdom

I

Wholeness, Simplicity and Profundity

One person who inspired me and gave me the courage to write a crazy book like this was Thomas Merton (1915-1968). Merton was a Trappist monk, a contemplative, a student of world religions and a prolific writer who became convinced that the depths of Christian (especially Catholic and Orthodox) spirituality resonated with the deeper aspects of religious experience in other traditions. He was intrigued by Taoism/Daoism and especially by Chuang Tzu/Zhuangzi. As an admirer of Zen he both corresponded with and met D.T. Suzuki and Thich Nhat Hanh.

If one word characterizes Chuang Tzu's thought for Merton, it is "Wisdom." Writing to John C. Wu, a Chinese American translator of the *Tao te Ching* and an admirer of Chuang Tzu, Merton confesses that, when it comes to Chuang Tzu, he has become "more and more struck by the profundity of his thought." The monk considers him "one of the great wise men." His wisdom "has a marvelous wholeness" which is simple but at the same time "utterly profound" (Merton, HGL, 613). Merton believed that God had "manifested His wisdom so simply and so strikingly in the early Chinese sages." Christians must have the humility "to learn and learn much, perhaps to acquire a whole new orientation of thought" from these ancient wisdoms and to strive earnestly to achieve a fulfillment of "spiritual wisdom" made possible through Christ (Ibid.).

Thomas Merton had the ability to read translations of the *Chuang Tzu* in several European languages. Drawing upon his own literary and contemplative sensitivities, Merton presents the reader with beautifully crafted selections from the *Chuang Tzu*. The core inner chapters of this ancient work were the product of the philosopher Chuang Tzu/Zhuangzi himself, as were many other selections scattered throughout the classic. The remainder were collected and/ or written by those in ancient China inspired by his thought as well as his unique mode of presentation.

Merton certainly found a deep resonance between his beloved Sophia (Wisdom) and Tao. In his now famous letter to artist Victor Hammer, Merton notes that Sophia as the Wisdom of God "is also the Tao, the nameless pivot of all being and nature, the center and meaning of all."

Like Tao, Sophia is the "feminine principle in the universe . . . the inexhaustible source of creative realization of the Father's glory in the world and is in fact the manifestation of that glory." As personified, she is also the "feminine child" who plays in and through Creation (Merton, WTF, 4).

Chuang Tzu himself displays the cosmic humility and playfulness of one who is aware of his place within the great mystery of the Way (Chinese landscape paintings capture something of this spirit). His wisdom, Merton claims, "manifests itself everywhere by a Franciscan simplicity and connaturality with all living creatures." In fact, "[h]alf of the 'characters' who are brought before us to speak the mind of Chuang Tzu are animals—birds, fishes, frogs, and so on." (Merton, WCT, 2). For Merton. this signifies Chuang Tzu's nostalgia for "the primordial climate of paradise" (Merton, WCT, 27).

Paradise "is still ours, but we do not know it," writes Merton, "since the effect of life in society is to complicate and confuse our existence, making us forget who we really are by causing us to be obsessed with what we are not" (Merton, WCT, 27). Both Merton and Chuang Tzu were very critical of those social forces that work against the full flourishing of and harmony between humans and the natural world. However, they both felt that we are capable, when freed from alienating social conventions, of acting "in perfect harmony with the whole" (Merton, WCT, 28).

Perhaps a new contemplative ecology is needed, one aware of the earth's marvelous wholeness, yet attuned to its diverse nuances: a human wisdom joined with Earth wisdom (Eco-Sophia). This wisdom would incorporate science while opening it up to its wider cosmic meaning and ecological relevance, and freeing it from its servitude to ideologies of domination and technologies of conquest. Merton draws upon his own contemplative experience and insights when he states that the natural world,

> . . . though "external" and "objective," is not something totally independent from us, which dominates us inexorably from without through the medium of certain fixed laws which science alone can discover and use. It is an extension of our lives, and if we attend to it respectfully, while attending also to our own freedom and our own integrity, we can learn to obey its ways and coordinate our lives with its mysterious movements. The way to find the real "world" is not merely to measure and observe what is outside us, but to discover our own inner ground. (Merton, CWA, 170)

Note that Merton suggests that we follow not the "laws" but the "ways" of nature and that we "coordinate our lives with its mysterious movements." We are being invited to a Taoist dance. Centered and free, flowing and responsive, we "discover [that] our own inner ground" opens out to a common ground. Like a tango, the human dance with nature will require us to "attend to it respectfully," respond to it sensitively, and with our more agile body, move with it grace-fully. Cook Ting dances with a live ox!

Therefore, the fundamental necessity for regaining a contemplative wisdom is to shake off the pathologies that distort our view of reality. Let elders, especially, take seriously Merton's invitation to learn from Chuang Tzu's Wisdom. Perhaps we can take a last look at how Chuang Tzu suggests we prepare our minds for an opening to Wisdom and Truth.

As the Franciscan Richard Rohr points out, "nondualistic thinking" as opposed to "both-and thinking" is a "calm and contemplative seeing" that appears more easily in the second half of life (Rohr, 146). For most people, such a contemplative seeing and nondualistic thinking were "put off or fully denied in the first half of life for the sake of quickly drawn ego boundaries and clear goals which created a nice, clean 'provisional personality'" (Rohr, 147). Chuang Tzu would agree with Rohr when the latter writes: "This calm allows you to confront what must be confronted with even greater clarity and incisiveness" (Ibid). And Rohr captures most of Chuang Tzu's characteristics of the dualistic mind: "it compares, it competes, it conflicts, it conspires, it condemns, it cancels out any contrary evidence and it then crucifies with impunity." He says we can call them the "seven C's of delusion, and the source of most violence . . ." (Rohr, 147).

Thus, one could say that when the human species, as one part of the whole, declares itself to be in charge of and imposes its will and its order upon the earth with its diverse species, chaos ensues. We inflict great pain when we divide the earth into the human and non-human, cling to the human and wage war on the non-human. We inflict pain when we force other life forms to conform to our narrow dualistic (us-them) vision of the earth. The frightening part is that we can do so with the best of intentions but with self-destructive results.

Chuang Tzu believed deeply in the immanent power of Tao to bring fullness and harmony to mind, heart and spirit. He did not divide reality into a deterministic realm called "nature" or "body" and a transcendent free realm called "spirit" or "mind." Rather, he held that the natural, the social, and the personal "ways" were capable of an integrated holism and modes of action when guided by the Way. Unfortunately, it has been the deterministic mechanism of the social machine—not Nature-- that has threatened personal freedom and interrupted the flow of Tao. Thus by reducing the uniquely inner *personal* to the collectively maneuvered *individual*, society has made creative and spontaneous expressions of wisdom difficult. Nature, for Taoists, is not the chaotic reign of the "law of the jungle." Rather, it is a harmonious and spontaneously functioning whole. The so-called "violence" of nature, usually short-lived and contained, was nothing compared to the biological, cultural, and psychological violence that could be visited over long periods and sometimes very brief moments in time on untold numbers of people by their fellow humans.

WORKS CITED

Merton, Thomas. *Contemplation in a World of Action.* Garden City, NY: Doubleday, 1971

_____ *The Hidden Ground of Love,* William H. Shannon, Ed. New York: Farrar, Straus, and Giroux, 1985.

_____. *The Way of Chuang Tzu.* New York: New Directions Publishing Corp., 1965.

_____. *Witness to Freedom: The Letters of Thomas Merton in Times of Crises.* William H. Shannon, editor. Harvest Books, 1995.

Rohr, Richard. *Falling Upward: A Spirituality for the Two Halves of Life.* San Francisco: Jossey-Bass, 2011.

GLOSSARY

WADE-GILES	PINYIN
Ch'i	Qi (breath, energy)
Ching	jing reverence
Chih	zhi wisdom
Chuang Tzu	Zhuangzi
Chun tzu	junzi gentleman, superior person
Ho	he harmony
hsin	xin (Heart-Mind) faithfulness
hsaio	xaio filial piety
hsueh	xin learning
I	yi rightness, duty, uprightness
Jen	ren humanity, humanness
Kung Fu/kungfu	gong fu/gongfu
Lao Tzu	Laozi

Li	li propriety, ritual
Lieh Tzu Liezi	Master Lie
Ming	ming fate, destiny
Shen	Shen spirit, person, body

T'ai chi ch'uan taijiquan	
Tao	dao (the way)
Te	De (integrity, virtue, moral power)
T'ien	Tian (heaven, Nature)
Ting, (cook)	Ding, (cook)
Wen	wen culture, Arts of peace
Wu	wu (nothing, no)
Wu hsin	wu xin (mindlessness)
Wu wei	wuwei (non-action)

yu	you (wandering, roaming)
yung	yong ordinary, common, the Mean
yung	yong courage

Printed in the United States
By Bookmasters